THE PRINCE OF WALES' EASTERN BOOK

THE PRINCE OF WALES' EASTERN BOOK

A PICTORIAL RECORD OF THE VOYAGES OF H.M.S. RENOWN, 1921-1922

SIR PERCIVAL PHILLIPS

GYAN

Published by

Gyan Publishing House
5, Ansari Road
Daryaganj, New Delhi-110002
Phone: 011-47034999, 9811692060
E-mail: books@gyanbooks.com

Distribution Network
gyanbooks.com
India, USA, Canada, UK, Australia

ISBN: 978-93-7447-022-0 (PB)

First Published, 1922

2nd Impression 2025

Printed at: Gyan Press, Delhi.

THE PRINCE OF WALES' EASTERN BOOK
Author: SIR PERCIVAL PHILLIPS

THE PRINCE OF WALES
EASTERN BOOK

THE PRINCE ARRIVES AT THE LAKE-SIDE PALACE, UDAIPUR

The Prince of Wales' Eastern Book

A PICTORIAL RECORD OF THE VOYAGES OF H.M.S. "RENOWN"
1921—1922

Published for St. Dunstan's
BY
Hodder and Stoughton, Limited
London New York Toronto

ST JAMES' PALACE,
S.W.1.

A second book of photographs this time illustrating my journey to India and The Far East, is being issued on behalf of The Blinded Soldiers' and Sailors' Hostel at St Dunstans'. I trust that the proceeds of it's sale will prove of considerable benefit to the most deserving object to which they are being devoted.

Edward P.

14.10.22.

ST. JAMES'S PALACE. S.W.

Introduction

THE Eastern tour of the Prince of Wales during 1921–22 was in many respects the most important mission his Royal Highness has yet undertaken in the interests of the Empire. Although, in point of distance travelled, it did not equal the tour to Australia and New Zealand—the journey by sea being, roughly, 8,000 miles less—it covered a wider and more varied field, and yielded an exhaustive survey of political and social conditions in the countries of Asia which are most directly concerned with the welfare of the British Empire.

The tour lasted eight months, and involved a journey by land and sea of nearly 41,000 miles. Four months was spent in India and one month in Japan. During the outward and homeward voyages, the Prince visited all the British possessions strung along the great highway between Gibraltar and the Pacific. He inaugurated the new Constitution at Malta, and saw the work accomplished by good government in such remote places as Aden and Borneo. He was the guest of the King of Egypt at Cairo and of the American government in the Philippines. He traversed India from sea to sea and from Madras to the borders of Afghanistan ; he travelled through the heart of Burma and into the mysterious kingdom of Nepal.

The Indian tour was divided into two parts, separated by the visit to Burma. The first half took his Royal Highness northward from Bombay through the native states of

Rajputana to Nepal and Calcutta, and the second half from Madras to Delhi and Peshawar, and then across the Sind desert to Karachi, the total distance travelled being about 8,200 miles.

As on his two previous Empire tours, the Prince travelled in the battle cruiser *Renown*, occupying with his personal staff the suite of cabins usually reserved for an admiral. For the short voyage from Calcutta to Burma, and thence back to Madras, he used the Royal Indian Marine troopship *Dufferin*. While in India, three special trains were put at his Royal Highness' disposal, and he changed from one to the other according to the gauge of the railway. The itinerary was so arranged that nearly all the journeys were made at night, thus enabling him to arrive early in the morning at his next destination. He also travelled by elephant, by palanquin, by camel, and in other unusual ways during his protracted pilgrimage through the East.

The staff which served with his Royal Highness on the tour was as follows :—

EUROPEAN STAFF.

Whole Tour (7)

Vice-Admiral Sir Lionel Halsey, G.C.V.O., K.C.M.G., C.B.
Sir Godfrey Thomas, Bart., C.V.O.
Captain Dudley North, C.M.G., C.V.O., R.N.
Captain The Hon. Piers Legh, M.V.O., O.B.E.
Lieutenant The Hon. Bruce Ogilvy, M.C.
Surgeon-Commander A. C. W. Newport, M.V.O., R.N.
Lieutenant The Lord Louis Mountbatten, M.V.O., R.N.

Trip out, India and Ceylon (1)

The Earl of Cromer, K.C.I.E., C.V.O.

Trip out and India (1)

Mr. G. F. de Montmorency, C.I.E., C.B.E., I.C.S

India (6)

Colonel-on-the-Staff R. B. Worgan, C.S.I., C.V.O., D.S.O.
Lieutenant-Colonel F. O'Kinealy, C.I.E., C.V.O., I.M.S.
Lieutenant-Colonel C. O. Harvey, C.V.O., C.B.E., M.C.
H. A. F. Metcalfe, Esq., M.V.O., I.C.S.
D. Petrie, Esq., C.I.E., C.V.O., C.B.E., Indian Police.
Captain F. S. Poynder, M.V.O., O.B.E., M.C.

India and rest of Tour (1)

Captain E. D. Metcalfe, M.C.

Ceylon and rest of Tour (1)

Brigadier-General C. R. Woodroffe, C.M.G., C.B.E.

Japan (1)

C. J. Davidson, Esq., C.I.E., C.V.O.

INDIAN PRINCES

India (10) *

Major-General H.H. The Maharaja of Patiala, G.C.S.I., G.C.I.E., G.C.V.O., G.B.E.
Lieutenant H.H. The Nawab of Bahawalpur, K.C.V.O.
Captain H.H. The Maharaja of Jodhpur, K.C.V.O.
Lieutenant-Colonel H.H. The Maharaj Rana of Dholpur, K.C.S.I. K.C.V.O.
H.H. The Maharaja of Dhar, K.C.S.I., K.C.V.O., K.B.E.
Colonel H.H. The Maharaja of Rutlam, K.C.S.I., K.C.V.O.
Captain H.H. The Nawab of Palanpur, K.C.I.E., K.C.V.O.
Captain Raja Sir Hari Singh of Kashmir, K.C.I.E., K.C.V.O
Captain The Maharaj Kumar of Bikaner, C.V.O.
Nawabzada Hamidullah Khan of Bhopal, C.V.O.

JAPANESE SUITE

Japan (9)

Count Sutomi Chinda, G.C.V.O., G.B.E.
Major-General Toyohiko Yoshida, K.C.V.O., C.B., C.M.G.
Mr. Nobumichi Sakenobe, K.B.E., C.I.E.
Rear-Admiral Katsunoshin Yamanashi, K.B.E., C.M.G.
Captain Shinjiro Yamamoto, K.B.E., C.V.O., C.B.E., I.J.N.
Commander Kai Kurokawa, C.V.O., I.J.N.
Viscount Keimin Matsudaira, C.V.O., C.B.E.
Lieutenant-Colonel Masanosuke Tsunoda, C.I.E., C.V.O., D.S.O.
Marquis Tsuneyasu Nakanomikado, C.V.O.

* 5 Indian Orderly Officers were also attached.

AMERICAN STAFF

Philippines Islands (2)

Major-General Omar Bundy
Captain Z. E. Briggs, U.S.N

TOTAL : 39

* 5 Indian Orderly Officers were also attached, bringing the tota up to 44.

The tour began on October 26, when the *Renown* left Portsmouth at sunset with her band playing "Auld Lang Syne," and the Prince looking down from his saluting platform above the bridge on an impressive and very moving farewell scene. Calls were made at Gibraltar, Malta, Port Said, Suez, and Aden. Bombay was reached on November 17. Four months later to a day, the *Renown* sailed again from Karachi for Japan. During the voyage the Prince paid visits to Ceylon, the Federated Malay States, the Straits Settlements, and Hong Kong. The homeward journey began at Kagoshima on May 9, and calls were made at Manila, Labuan, Jesselton and Brunei (Borneo), Penang, Trincomalee, Great Hamish (for oil), Suez (whence his Royal Highness went to Cairo), and Gibraltar. The *Renown* arrived at Plymouth late on the afternoon of June 20, and the Prince proceeded to London by special train next morning.

ST. JAMES' PALACE,
S.W. 1.

H.R.H. THE PRINCE OF WALES desires to express his gratitude to Messrs. HODDER & STOUGHTON for undertaking the publication of a second book of this nature; to the CENTRAL NEWS for permission to reproduce their copyright photographs; to Mr. DONALD MAXWELL for his kindness in providing the delightful paintings; and to Sir PERCIVAL PHILLIPS for writing the Narrative of the Tour.

GIBRALTAR : INDIA BURMA

THE third morning after leaving Portsmouth, the *Renown* anchored at Gibraltar. The "Rock" had put on gala dress, and the little fortress town welcomed the Prince joyfully when he came ashore at Ragged Staff. East and West met in the narrow main street through which he drove to Government House. Grave Moors from the African coast ; Spaniards from beyond the wire-bound frontier at Linea, and from Algeciras, across the bay, hardy sailor men from the merchant ships in harbour ; nuns, dockyard hands, Hindu merchants, and priests mingled with the garrison folk and sounded the first note of an ovation that was to take him half-way round the world and back. The tall buildings in the high street were masked with gay tapestries and carpets of vivid hues draped Spanish fashion from the window ledges, whence eager faces peered at the little procession below. The Prince saw it all with an appreciative eye, but the leaven of khaki that is the real foundation of the "Rock" held his gaze longest. Here were old comrades of the Western front, the fourth battalion of the "Die Hards" of Middlesex, of which he is colonel-in-chief, lately arrived at this gateway to the East. They were his guard of honour for the day, and the fact pleased him greatly. He met them first at the jetty and again in the afternoon when he inspected the battalion at Buena Vista barracks.

The day was spent informally with the varied population of Gibraltar. He received addresses from the Exchange Committee, the Chamber of Commerce, and the Workers' Union. The school children, boy scouts, girl guides, and police were inspected at Alameda parade ground, and a garden party at Government House brought his Royal Highness in touch with other elements of the community. He found time to inspect the oil tanks and the entrance to the Admiralty Tunnel at Monkey's Quarry. In the evening he gave a dinner party on board.

When the *Renown* left the inner anchorage at 10 p.m., with the *Calypso*, her escorting cruiser, showing the way to sea, the last view of Gibraltar was very beautiful. All the warships in harbour were festooned with lights and the buildings huddled on the lower slope of the "Rock" made a prodigal display of electric lamps. As the Prince's battle cruiser headed for the Mediterranean, the long harbour walls burst into flame. Red, white, and blue flares, swung by well-trained dockyard hands, signalled farewell in rapid changes of colour combinations, while the rugged outline of the "sleeping lion"—the crest of the fortress as seen against the sky—awoke in the darkness under the white glare of searchlights.

Two days were spent at Malta. The Mediterranean Fleet, headed by the flagship *Iron Duke*, led the welcome that ushered the *Renown* into the Grand Harbour at Valetta early on November 1, and from every wall and jetty and housetop overlooking the anchorage came the cheers of the loyal Maltese. The most important duty performed by the Prince at Malta was the inauguration of the new Constitution on the morning of his arrival. He drove from the jetty to the Governor's palace, formerly the residence of the Grand Master of the Knights of Malta, and there, in the Hall of St. Michael and George, he was received by the members of the new Senate and the lower house at 11 o'clock. Lord Plumer, the Governor, read the King's Commission, after which His Royal Highness made a short speech declaring the Parliament open. The streets of Valetta were packed with excited people, to whom the establishment of a Legislature meant the beginning of a new era in the history of their island. They cheered like a London crowd as the Prince passed and re-passed through the city; when he visited St. John's Cathedral, which is bound up with the history of the Knights; when he drove to the Casino Maltese to lunch, and then to a garden party at San Antonio Palace; when he went to a performance of "Aida" at the Opera House, and even at midnight on his going on to a dance at the Naval Commander-in-Chief's residence.

Next day he came even closer to the people of Valetta. In the morning he received a memorable ovation from the dockyard employees when he went over the naval establishment and physical training school. In the afternoon they cheered him as a sportsman when he appeared at a gymkhana as one of the competitors in an amusing "King's Messenger" race. It was a strangely mixed effort, in which the Prince enacted the part of the "Messenger." He had first to run in a sack for 20 yards; then ride 100 yards on a bareback mule; then be carried 50 yards on a stretcher; mount a pony and ride 50 yards; be wheeled in a barrow for another 20 yards, and then be driven for a final 100 yards in a native vehicle known as a "carozzia." The Prince was only beaten after a grim struggle. The race caused intense merriment which he fully shared.

The *Renown* took a longer time to pass through the Suez Canal than an ordinary ship, owing to her great size and draught. She arrived at Port Said early in the afternoon of November 5, and did not enter the "ditch" until next morning. The Prince went ashore for a two hours' ride along the sea front, and in the evening he gave a dinner party on board, the guests including high British and Egyptian officials from Cairo. The journey from Port Said to the Bitter Lakes, which was made so slowly that horsemen on the banks were able to keep pace with the ship, took his Royal Highness past the familiar camps of El Kantara and Ismailia, which were important bases for the military operations in Palestine. The troops remaining there gathered at the water's edge to cheer him on his way ; and the calm of Sunday was broken repeatedly by their noisy greetings. Here the Prince had his first sight of Indian troops during the tour. The climax came at the entrance to the Bitter Lake, where the population of Ismailia, massed on a steep sandy bluff, shouted itself hoarse as the *Renown* passed to her resting-place for the night. Next morning the ship resumed her slow, cautious progress between two watchful tugs, and at 5 o'clock came into the broad roadstead at Suez. There she remained twenty-four hours. The Prince landed twice at Port Tewfik for long rides in the desert.

The barren hills of Aden lay before the *Renown* on the morning of November 12. To the majority of travellers, Aden seems the bleakest, most desolate spot in the British Empire, and a great deal of pity is bestowed upon its unfortunate inhabitants. It would have been difficult, however, to find happier, more cheerful subjects of the King than these self-same exiles when they assembled along the narrow strip of sea front beside the jetty to see their Prince. The arid, treeless town, an aching wilderness devoid of even a single scrap of green foliage, had been covered with bright flags and streamers, and the very rocks were splashed with colour. British and Indian infantry were waiting to be inspected on a sun-baked parade

ARRIVAL OF THE PRINCE'S WHITE CAR THROUGH THE STRANGE CLEFT (ADEN)

ground, and a crowd that embraced many colours and creeds acclaimed the Prince with a single voice.

Four dignified chiefs from the mysterious country behind Aden were waiting for him at Government House on the hill. They were brought up, one after the other, in the shadows of a cool, wide veranda, and presented in phrases of stately Arabic. None of them is known beyond the Gulf of Aden, but all of them faced their future King-Emperor with fine dignity. Even their names, recited in sonorous tones by the interpreter, brought up visions of an Eastern court. Came first Sir Abdul Karim bin Fadl bin Ali (the Adali), a tall, erect figure in gold brocade, striding forward with one hand on his jewelled sword, his little son beside him ready to read an address in nervous, halting English ; then the aged Sultan Husein bin Ahmed (the Fadli), who is nearly a century old and almost blind, drawing his purple robe around him as he groped forward on the arm of a sleek frock-coated chamberlain of his desert court ; then the Sultan Abdul Kadir bin Husein, his son ; and, last of all, the Amir Nasr bin Shaif Sef of Dali, lean, lithe, very composed, disdaining jewelled ornaments, his bare feet, tipped with henna, thrust forward from a gown of dull green silk.

The Prince saw all of Aden. He drove to the Crater, passing children of the Government and Jewish schools, who sang the National Anthem in Arabic, Hebrew, and Somali ; he met the 1st Battalion Yemen Infantry—sturdy soldiers recruited from desert tribes—and interviewed a group of Somali chiefs from the African hinterland, who were waiting for him by the famous Tawela tanks. Then the entire population surged back to the harbour front to watch his Royal Highness re-embark, and when the *Renown* steamed into the Indian Ocean, at 5 o'clock, he could see thousands of friendly salutes signalled from the ragged rocks.

The *Renown's* voyage across an unruffled sea ended on November 17, when, at sunrise, the guns of the British East Indies squadron and the French cruiser *d'Este* saluted her in the harbour of Bombay. At 10 o'clock the Prince of Wales first set foot in the Indian Empire. His barge swung alongside the Apollo Bandar, where the Viceroy awaited him, and he passed through the imposing Gateway of India—a lofty, unfinished arch at the water-side—to a crowded amphitheatre beyond. Here, in the presence of a glittering assemblage, he stood under a silken canopy, on a carpet of cloth of gold, and read the King's Message. The state procession, with its escort of scarlet cavalry, carried him through five miles of beflagged streets from the modern European city into a residential quarter fully mobilized in his honour, and thence to Government House at the end of Malabar Point. The obvious sincerity of the welcome on the route was in striking contrast with the disaffection revealed elsewhere. The rioting in the bazaars, that necessitated the employment of armoured cars, never extended beyond the limits of the Indian quarter. The Prince heard no discordant note in the rejoicing, saw no sign of hostility in the faces around him. This was true not only of his first journey through Bombay, but of all other appearances there in public as well. He went about freely outside the native city, fulfilling a programme that was in no wise affected by the pressure of political agitators. He walked through a dense throng of Indians on the Maidan—a great open space skirting the European quarter—with no more apparent precautions than might be taken to secure him elbow-room in a London crowd.

The Bombay programme was a typical example of the duties undertaken by his Royal Highness throughout the Indian itinerary. Invariably on this tour he met the ex-service men and pensioners; the British and Indian troops of local garrisons and of the forces maintained by native princes; boy scouts, girl guides, police, and other civic and military organizations. Each town was a rallying point for wide areas, and during his four months' journey the Prince met most of the soldiers—past and present—that have been identified with the military history of the Indian Empire for a generation. At Bombay, as elsewhere, he was attended by his staff of Indian Princes, and this close association yielded valuable knowledge of the States that are knit together with British India. He had his first interviews with other important rulers at Government House. He visited the University, the Seamen's Institute, and the Yacht Club; presented colours to the 7th Rajputs on the Maidan in the presence of a vast crowd, and witnessed a fine naval and military pageant which followed the final cricket match of the quadrangular tournament between teams representing the Presidency and the Parsees. On the day of his departure, he was present at the exciting final match of the commemoration polo tournament between the Maharaja of Rutlam's team and that of the Universities. Rutlam won by 5 goals to 3, and the Prince presented cups to the winners and runners-up.

His stay in Bombay was broken by a one-day visit to Poona, the centre of Mahratta tradition and sentiment. His Royal Highness made the journey there and back at night. The few hours spent in the Deccan capital brought him in touch with some of the most powerful native rulers in that part of India, and gave him his first glimpse of the gorgeous ceremonial of native India. The main object of the visit was to lay the foundation stones of two memorials which appeal powerfully to all Mahrattas. Immediately on his arrival, his Royal Highness drove from the railway station by a circuitous route to the

Shanwar Wada Gate, where the memorial to Mahrattas who fell in the war will be erected. Thence he was taken with great pomp to another part of Poona where he laid the foundation stone of the memorial to Shivaji, founder of the last great Empire, and the hero of all Mahrattas. Jewelled and painted elephants saluted his state barouche as he passed with an escort of Gwalior Lancers from the site of one memorial to the other. Descendants of the nobles of the Mahratta dominion awaited him in pavilions beside a Royal dais, and 10,000 people witnessed his arrival. The nobles were in traditional state dress, with curiously draped and embroidered skirts, and stiff, flat, cocked hats of crimson silk; their forearms were encased in gold plates, and at their side hung a short jewelled sword. Two Maharajas—Scindia of Gwalior, and Kolhapur, the latter a massive figure in white surmounted by a purple puggaree, a great man in the district, and regarded by Mahrattas with awe—led the Prince to his throne. He laid the foundation stone with mortar spread from a gold basin, and all the multitude shouted: "Prince ki jai." Mahratta chiefs, ranging in age from old men to a proud dignified boy, who went through his part with nonchalant ease, filed past the dais offering his Royal Highness gold garlands, betel nut, and scent from gold salvers.

All formality was dispensed with in the afternoon. Poona saw the Prince as a keen sportsman, intent on the races at the Western India Turf Club. He presented cups, walked among the crowd, was cheered repeatedly by thousands of people, and came back to his special train at 7 o'clock leaving the happiest of impressions.

The Prince left Bombay finally on the night of November 21, driving to Victoria terminus station in a flood of light. All the public buildings were illuminated and the streets through which he passed were filled with cheering people.

BARODA

The first stage of the tour northwards took his Royal Highness through six independent States, each with its own distinct atmosphere and traditions. He saw the " New India " as exemplified by Baroda with its bustling English-speaking officials, modern art gallery, lending libraries, social " uplift " work for the submerged classes, and European architecture. Then he slipped back into the Middle Ages at Udaipur which boasts proudly that it is to-day as it was four centuries ago. He struck off into the desert to Bikaner, that remote yet very progressive capital surrounded by a waste of sand, where camels are as common as omnibuses in a London street. The highest compliment one Prince could pay him—a Prince who claims direct descent from the Sun—was to have him carried in a palanquin, surrounded by torchbearers when he went to dine in state. Another Prince struck the modern note by importing especially for his visit an entire fleet of Rolls-Royce cars. One host is reputed to be the best polo player in India ; another would as soon think of undressing in the main street as of knocking a ball about in competition with other men. Thus, the native States that lay on his route from Bombay to Nepal and Calcutta offered a varied, sometimes an almost bewildering succession of contrasts, but their rulers were animated by the same desire : to outdo each other in the lavishness and magnificence of the entertainments organised by them for the future King-Emperor.

Baroda came first. The Gaekwar met his Royal Highness at the railway station the morning after the departure from Bombay, and they drove together with an imposing escort of State troops through clean, wide streets filled with the Gaekwar's people. Their houses and shops were covered with flags and messages of welcome in English. Fifteen thousand school children divided into eight groups—including the so-called " untouchable " classes—helped dress the route, and screened stands were filled with " purdah " ladies gazing eagerly at the pageant. Gilded elephants salaamed outside the Law Courts; at Laxmi Vilas Palace, gold and silver cannon and state carriages of solid silver, harnessed to horses in cumbersome trappings, were drawn up beside the guard of honour. When the Prince went a little later from Laxmi Vilas to Nazar Bag Palace—a plain white building in pleasant grounds, not unlike an English country house—to return the Gaekwar's call, he found more evidences of Baroda's splendour. In a small ante-room were displayed £3,000,000 worth of diamonds and pearls, including a diamond once worn by Napoleon III, and purchased in Paris in 1867. The Gaekwar gave an afternoon party in the grounds of Laxmi Vilas which offered strange and varied entertainment. Elephants in full court dress were available for those who cared to ride them, and a " Director of Amusements " presided over an exhibition of acrobats, performing birds, native plays, songs and dances, arranged in open booths around a level stretch of lawn. The Gaekwar had searched all India to provide the finest performers for a single hour. The state banquet in the evening was held in the grand hall of Laxmi Vilas Palace, and on this occasion the first public announcement was made of the engagement of Princess Mary.

The Prince went into the country early next morning to watch a cheetah hunt, and saw one buck killed. He left in the afternoon for Udaipur, stopping two hours at Rutlam *en route* to dine with the Maharaja. Rutlam was illuminated as though for a week's visit. The Maharaja lavished electric lamps on his palace and public buildings, and the inhabitants of the capital waited *en masse* during dinner to see his guest drive back to the train.

UDAIPUR

Three days were spent in the lovely lakeside capital of Mewar State. Old travellers regretted that this visit could not have been kept for the end of the tour. The beauty of Udaipur, the picturesqueness of its buildings and site; its aloofness from the twentieth century and tenacious hold on the past; and its preservation from the devastating influence of casual tourists combine to give it a position unique among the cities of India. The Maharana's massive fortress-like palace rises above a placid lake studded with little island pavilions of white marble. The streets are crooked, and the tumble-down bazaars seem to have lasted miraculously through many generations of Rajput Princes. Elephants wander through the outer palace yard; fierce retainers shouldering matchlocks, or fingering jewelled swords, stride through the main gate. Europeans are still met with polite salaams, as formerly they were throughout India, and the doctrines of Gandhi receive no consideration in the market place. Life pursues its slow, untroubled way and the years make no impression on the Maharana's court. There is nothing else between Madras and the Northern Passes quite like Udaipur. The traveller who goes there first is likened to a man who begins a banquet with the chef's masterpiece, and is troubled to find the other dishes rather dull.

The Prince left his broad gauge "special" at Rutlam junction, and changed to a smaller Royal train for the journey to Udaipur. The devious branch line crawls painfully through rock and scrub and ends finally three miles from the capital. The Maharana will not have a railway profaning the city of his fathers. The twentieth century stops at the 3-mile limit, and those who yearn for the travel facilities of the western world had better turn back when they reach the dead end called Udaipur station.

The league stretch of road leading to the city was

guarded by feudal chiefs from all parts of Mewar and their wild followers, all mounted and armed, sitting motionless on their fine Arab horses, their matchlocks, many of which were inlaid in gold and silver, held stiffly upright. At intervals were posted standard bearers carrying aloft bright coloured banners, and drummers pounding steadily on enormous drums lashed athwart their saddles. There were Bhils among them—the shy savage little men of whom Kipling writes—and graceful, straight-backed youths, heirs of the lesser lords of Rajputana, and proud, whiskered, old warriors who rule in obscure corners of the State. The foot soldiers of the Maharana, variously uniformed, and more variously armed, kept the intervening spaces, and behind them were the staring inhabitants of the bazaars banked against the city walls, hanging over the battlements, even peering down from trees at the Prince who had come from another world. The open field where elephants drugged into frenzy used to fight before the Maharana's court was occupied by ancient cannon hidden in the smoke of their old fashioned salute.

The Prince spent three days in Udaipur. He visited the island palaces in Jagmandir Lake, saw the wild pigs fed at Odi-khas, and wandered through the bazaars. Even in this remote place ex-service men were gathered to greet him. He shot snipe on Pichola Lake, and enjoyed a lively dance by Bhils at the British Residency. The most vivid impression of his stay was the scene on the first night when he went by barge down Jagmandir Lake to the state banquet at the palace. All the city was outlined in innumerable little oil lamps, and the island pavilions were like dream palaces rising out of a silver sea. Along the water front crouched the silent, intent, population—dark masses seen dimly against the flickering lights behind ; they framed the bathing ghats and quays, and formed a ghostly living frieze on the roofs of the lakeside temples. The lighting of Udaipur on this night was conceived by a great artist. All the city seemed steeped in a golden glow, save only the grim, harsh bulk of the citadel, and this the master's hand had left in darkness save for a single thin band of white drawn cleanly across the high flat roof and sides—a simple frame for a picture such as Brangwyn might have etched. The Prince was carried in a chair up the steep winding footway from the water gate to the banqueting hall. He was hatless, and the memory of this fair-haired youth ascending in silence with his dusky bearers against the heavy, windowless façade of the Maharana's mysterious palace, with all the night aflame around him is one that will not be soon forgotten.

His host was a fitting figure in this Eastern scene. He is old and fragile, but despite the illness that prevented him from welcoming the Prince at the railway station that morning, his personality dominated, almost oppressively, the gathering over which he presided. Tall, gaunt, with the clear cut features of a Rajput noble, and calm, keen eyes, he saluted his guests with wonderful dignity. His thin, white beard was clipped and brushed squarely across his hollow cheeks ; he wore his brilliant robe with the air of a reigning sovereign, and the little court assembled around him plainly felt the majesty of this descendant of the Sun.

He did not eat with the assembled company. After all the guests had been welcomed he retired, as orthodox Indian Princes do on such an occasion, until the banquet was finished, when he returned to make a stately little speech of welcome. Then the Prince of Wales went with him to Minto Hall where, on a balcony high above the lake, they witnessed a display of fireworks that seemed to engulf all the buildings of the fairy city in a torrent of fire.

The departure from Udaipur was marked by the same display of Rajput clans and drummers. The Maharaj-kumar (Heir Apparent) drove with his Royal Highness to the frontier of the twentieth century, and at sunset on November 27 the special train left again for British India. Next morning he was at Ajmer. This pleasant town is a kind of British "island" surrounded by native States, for here the Agent to the Governor-General for Rajputana has his headquarters. It is a place of pilgrimage, for the Sacred lake of Pushkar, noted for its Hindu Temple, is only a few miles distant, and on this day the streets adjoining the main bazaar were filled with little groups of half-naked, ash-smeared faquirs or " holy men," sitting in the dust surrounded by their adoring disciples. The Prince drove in semi-state to the Ana Saga Bund, a terrace overlooking the site of an ancient lake—now dry—where a number of ruling and minor chiefs and princes did homage in one of the marble pavilions built by the Emperor Shah Jehan. The remainder of the day was devoted to an inspection of pensioners, the distribution of prizes at Mayo College, tennis, and a dinner party at the Residency.

The Prince found an old friend waiting for him at Jodhpur next morning in the person of the late Sir Pratap Singh, the Maharaja Regent, who served in France with the Indian Corps. He ruled Jodhpur in the name of the young Maharaja with a wise, strong hand, and his influence has repeatedly been felt for good during periods of unrest. He built a wonderful camp at the gate of the modern palace where the Prince was lodged for three days, and furnished it sumptuously for this brief visit. A great shamiana or reception tent, lined with silken draperies, was the Durbar Hall, for the exchange of official visits between the Mahajara Regent and his guest. Two gilt thrones set on gold tapestry were placed for them at one end. Beyond was a still larger loftier tent hung in blue and white, where the state banquet took place. From these central structures radiated streets of residential tents, each a suite of luxuriously furnished apartments complete even to telephones and reading lamps. The construction of this miniature canvas town took weeks ; it served its purpose in three nights and was demolished. On such a scale did the Princes of India entertain the Prince of Wales.

The principal sport at Jodhpur was pig-sticking. His Royal Highness went out two mornings before breakfast, accompanied by Sir Pratap Singh, who, despite his 77 years was as keen and active as the youngest members of the party. The Prince speared the first pig on the first morning, and the total bag was five on the first day, and eleven on the second. Before leaving Jodhpur he reviewed the Jodhpur Lancers who were the last Imperial Service troops to leave France. Six squadrons went past in magnificent style, and his Royal Highness shook hands with the officers, and distributed decorations.

Another night's journey brought him to Bikaner on the morning of December 2. From Jodhpur the Royal train crawled through the desert, watched and guarded by camel patrols. Whenever the Prince looked from his window he could see the lonely figures of these sentinels silhouetted against the moonlit sky. They sat rigidly on their camels, at intervals of perhaps 200 yards, and as the train passed each man held aloft a flare. A message could have been flashed by word of mouth or uplifted torch from one capital to another while the Prince slept. The corridor across the sandy plain was lighted for him all through the night, and dawn revealed more guards, increasing in number, until the city was reached. In a similar way the Prince's progress up and down India was always patrolled by soldiers and police. There was never a moment during any journey by train, from the time he left Bombay on November 22, until he arrived at Karachi on March 17, when he could not see these vigilant watchers strung along the permanent way within hail of each other, usually with their backs to the train, and their eyes fixed on the fields or jungle. The fine discipline of the Indian troops was shown by their strict compliance with the order not to turn and look at the train. Their duty was to watch the country round about. The longing to steal one backward glance at the son of the British Raj, or at least to see his saloon must have been almost irresistible, but it was never betrayed save sometimes by an anxious twitching of the head, or an almost laughable attempt of some sentries to turn their eye-balls at right angles.

Five days were spent at Bikaner. All the ceremonial of the visit was compressed into the first day, and the remainder of the time left free for sport. The Maharaja himself is one of the best big game shots in India, and his palace of Lalgarh—a handsome modern structure of red sandstone, equipped with every European comfort—contains many paintings depicting his success in the jungle. His subjects came from all parts of the desert kingdom to see the fine pageant prepared for the Prince's reception. Seldom has there been such a gathering of camels. One saw camels everywhere : military camels with war service ; civilian camels concerned with government transport ; palace camels ; country camels, sniffing uneasily at the crowded streets and longing for the desert ; weatherworn C-3 camels in humble trappings sneering at their more gorgeous brethren—camels on all sides arching their necks and eyeing the unusual scene a little disdainfully. Their riders were very gorgeous. The sirdars wore silk robes of every imaginable hue, from rose-pink to vivid green, and the wealthier ones sported tunics covered with precious stones. They lined one side of the road, and their retainers the other, for a distance of two miles. The famous Bikaner Camel Corps was the Royal escort. It closed in around the barouche, where the Prince sat with the Maharaja, and moved off in fours with stately step into the crowded streets. Elephants in the usual fancy dress and " dazzle " paint, waited the cavalcade in a large square—for once they were a secondary feature of interest and the camels seemed to know it. Bullock teams with silver plated horns and covered with gaudy trailing mantles, had drawn archaic state carriages to this open space where they could add to the splendour of the picture. The entire population of the city lined the roadway, and even a contingent of the " untouchable " castes added its pitiful note to the welcome of the masses.

The etiquette of an Indian Court provides for certain ceremonies on the arrival of a Royal guest which were followed in every native State visited by the Prince of Wales. Soon after he reached his apartments, four officers of the Maharaja's household would arrive to inquire formally after his health—the ceremony known as " Mizaj-pursi." A little later four members of the Prince's suite returned the compliment. Another interval, and then the Maharaja went in state to call on the Prince, being received in a Durbar Hall where they sat side by side on a dais, with their respective suites ranged at right angles on either side of the room, and exchanged polite remarks as though they had met for the first time. Before leaving, the Maharaja and his followers received the customary offerings of itr and pan, and garlands of gold thread were hung about their necks. An hour or so later the Prince drove in state to return the visit. Again, he and his host sat together, while the officials and nobles of the State came forward singly to the dais with a low obeisance and proffered gold mohurs wrapped in white silk for the Prince to touch and remit. The Maharaja offered itr and pan from the state vessels held by court officials, and hung a garland over the Prince's head. The members of the Prince's suite were similarly decorated by dignitaries of the court. The setting for these visits varied from State to State, but the ceremony itself was almost invariably the same. At Bikaner, the homage of the Maharaja's government was paid in the Fort—the ancient palace—where the Prince was ushered with impressive ritual into a lofty pillared hall of rich, red stone, the upper walls of which were covered with broad screens of delicate, lace-like tracery thrown from balcony to balcony.

There is an old and a new Bikaner. The bulk of the population lives within high walls, in picturesque tumble-down houses, composing a labyrinth of crooked streets through which the usual traffic of an Eastern bazaar is constantly passing to the busy market place. Two miles distant is a well-planned modern city spread with lavish disregard for space over the plain. The Maharaja has put up government offices and schools on a scale that would do credit to any Western community; the buildings are of red sandstone, connected by broad avenues, and the uniformity of their design is very pleasing. There is a park with artificial lakes, and green turf which must surprise the dwellers in the desert; even the club which his Highness has built for the European colony is an imposing structure which is part of a harmonious and striking architectural scheme.

A military review and a state banquet completed the Prince's "ceremonial day." Six squadrons of the Camel Corps, a camel battery, cavalry of the bodyguard, lancers and a regiment of infantry passed before him on the parade ground in the new city. The banquet took place in the

Fort, where the Durbar Hall of the morning had been transformed into a dining hall. Upon its conclusion, the Prince was taken to another part of the old palace to see a very unusual spectacle. First, he witnessed a "fire dance" in the inner courtyard. Old men sat beside a great pile of glowing embers, beating drums and chanting, while some twenty devotees of the fire goddess capered and jumped around the pyre. As the music grew faster, their frenzy increased until they darted through the fire instead of around it, and scattered the glowing fragments with their naked feet. They even thrust fragments of burning wood into their mouth, and seemed to suffer no hurt, although the spectators could not hold the charred embers with comfort.

In another court the Prince witnessed nautch dances for the first time. An orchestra of strange instruments, some of which were as tall as an ordinary man, ushered in a procession of dancing women ranging in age from twelve to thirty. They moved slowly in ankle-length costumes of heavy silk, displaying tinkling silver ornaments on their bare feet. Their jet-black hair was plastered down tightly on either side of their forehead, and their eyes were blackened with "kohl." The orchestra crouching in the shadows wailed steadily, and the women swayed and postured to the monotonous music and sang patriotic songs. Then jugglers danced on naked swords. The Prince and the Maharaja, sitting in a balcony watched a scene that might have been taken bodily from the "Arabian Nights." The colonnaded marble court, open to the stars, was bathed in the mellow light of countless lamps; a fountain played at one end, and the air was heavy with scent. The intrusion of solemn attendants bearing trays of whisky and soda seemed little less than sacrilege.

The next day, December 3, the Prince went to Gujner, one of the Maharaja's palaces, twenty miles from Bikaner, and remained three days shooting imperial sand grouse. On the first drive his Royal Highness bagged 35, the highest amount by any single member of the party, and the total day's bag was 1,035. He also shot demoiselle crane at Kodamdesar.

The last State in Rajputana visited by the Prince during the journey to Nepal was Bharatpur, where he arrived on the morning of December 7. He played polo the first afternoon, and was considerably astonished when his host drove to the polo ground in a silver carriage harnessed to eight elephants. A night pageant at Bharatpur, which cost £60,000, was one of the most unusual features of the tour. The Maharaja had a hill built especially as the foundation for a pavilion from which his guests could watch the show in comfort. The plain in front was the stage. A low wall of earth formed the edge of it, and served as a screen for the "footlights." In the strong glare thrown by these hidden lamps, the native troops of Bharatpur State were revealed with striking effect as they marched out of the darkness across the "stage" and vanished again into the night. It was like an animated unending frieze unrolling smoothly to the gay music of an unseen band. Golden elephants cheerfully swinging their trunks gave way to camels sixteen abreast, then scarlet infantry marching like a guards battalion; dancing horses, native pipers, palanquins, and lumbering "purdah" carriages drawn by elephants, cavalry, a mournful lion cub in a cage, a miniature "tank" drawing half a dozen limbers, a small boy in a cart drawn by two antelopes, field kitchens, and—a column of Rolls Royce cars! The cavalry did a musical ride in and out of a maze of lighted lamps set on the ground, other horsemen rode standing through an

THE WONDERFUL CITY OF UDAIPUR

intricate pattern of flares. It was the military tournament at Olympia in a strange and beautiful setting.

From Bharatpur, the Prince went to Lucknow for five days. He was entertained by the Taluqdars of Oudh (the wealthy land-owners of the province), he reviewed the garrison ; visited King George's hospital ; rode in four events of a gymkhana, winning two and finishing second in the other two ; saw the poor fed in Victoria Park ; presented colours to the 3rd Worcesters, and spent a memorable Sunday afternoon at the ruins of the Residency, listening to stories of the siege. He left Lucknow on December 11 and spent a day each at Allahabad and Benares before proceeding to Nepal. At Allahabad he visited the University and the High Court, and met the landowners at Government House. His day at Benares was very interesting. The Maharaja met him at the cantonment railway station, and after the usual ceremonial visits, his Royal Highness drove in state from Nagwa Ghat to the University escorted by Benares Lancers. The students awaited him in a temporary amphitheatre in the University grounds facing a canopied dais, where the Prince was clothed by the Chancellor in the red and yellow robe of a Doctor ot Laws. He himself placed on his head the yellow puggaree which is part of the official dress, and this little incident greatly pleased the students. They cheered him with unexpected enthusiasm.

The Maharaja gave a luncheon for the Prince in an open courtyard of the old palace at Fort Ramnagar. The guests sat under a colonnade, and a band on the roof played Western airs. In the afternoon he went in a motor launch down the Ganges, past the temples and burning ghats to the landing place at Rajghat. He inspected the pensioners in their camp, visited an exhibition of local industries, and at 7.20 p.m. left for Nepal.

The week in Nepal was devoted to big game, chiefly tiger and rhinoceros. Very elaborate preparations had been made by the Maharaja Prime Minister and Marshal, to ensure good sport. He came down from Khatmandhu, the secluded capital beyond the passes, with various nobles and high officials of state, and superintended the erection of the Royal camp at the edge of the jungle, about a mile from the frontier of British India, and adjoining the railway terminus at Bikna Thori. Nepalese were drafted from all parts of the kingdom to clear this site, and to rebuild a road that would give access to some thirty miles of jungle. They came from the wilds with their kukris and cooking pots, and for weeks were busy making everything ready for the Prince. The game, in which Nepal abounds, was shepherded adroitly towards the selected preserve. Gurkha signallers loaned by the military authorities at Rawalpindi laid down telephone wires and signal posts along the new highway. H.H. Sir Shum Shere Jung's magic caused four perfectly equipped camps to appear in a dense forest, where, until a few weeks previously, wild elephant and tiger roamed at will. Only two days before the Royal party arrived, a herd of elephants came to the edge of the clearing, attracted by the lights, and seemed inclined to rush the stockade.

The Prince's camp was pitched in a patch of woodland on a bluff above a rocky river bed. The streets of tents were grouped around a central drawing-room and dining-room. They included offices for the secretaries and clerks who were always at work, whether travelling or in camp; a post office with a special telegraph wire to the outside world; and every comfort which the Nepalese could procure. There was even a tower of refuge against wild elephants: a platform level with the upper branches of the surrounding trees, supported on ponderous baulks of timber with a light stairway leading to the top. The Nepalese court had its own camp a quarter of a mile away; while somewhat nearer was an auxiliary camp for a portion of the Royal party, and one for the British Envoy to Nepal.

The Prince lost no time in exploring the jungle. His train arrived at Bikna Thori at 10 a.m. on December 14, and he motored across a rock-strewn valley into Nepal, a journey of less than fifteen minutes by motor car. An arch of green boughs spanned the roadway just within the frontier, where a guard of honour of Gurkhas awaited him, and priests from Khatmandhu performed a brief religious rite. An hour later the Prince was on his way to his first tiger hunt. A 9½ feet specimen had been "ringed" early that morning and the elephant cordon was waiting in the jungle. The Prince hit the tiger first and it was despatched by a member of his staff.

The procedure for each day's shoot was very simple. Buffaloes were tethered to stakes at nightfall, at likely places in the jungle, and early next morning the little Gurkha scouts made the rounds to see what had happened. If they found a stake and only part of a buffalo or no buffalo where there had been both a stake and a complete buffalo the night before, it was safe to assume that a gorged tiger was sleeping heavily in the tall grass several hundred yards away. The spot was immediately "picketed" by a few elephants, and the "kill" reported from the nearest telephone post to the Nepalese camp. By 10 a.m. "headquarters" had received reports from all parts of the jungle area marked out for the week's operations. The Royal party started in motor cars and went as near as possible along the road—the only road, by the way—to the "kill." As it was usually still some miles distant, the Prince and his companions mounted pad elephants—sitting on a pile of roped blankets—and when within a mile or two of the quarry, changed to howdahs. By this time a circle of perhaps one hundred elephants standing closely together had been formed around the sleeping tiger. The howdahs were assigned various positions as part of the circle, and then beaters went on foot into the jungle with trumpets and shrill cries. The din was terrific. The tiger, suddenly awakened from his lethargy, usually showed an intense desire to remain under cover. The greater the noise, the greater his determination to avoid publicity. Sometimes he would dart into the open in an angry bewildered fashion, only to bolt back again into the grass at the first glimpse of the cordon. Sooner or later however, he would be extracted. Perhaps a chance shot would sting him into fury, or sheer terror cause him to dash blindly forward. The nearest elephants would squeal nervously, fearing a charge. Sometimes the prisoner did leap on a howdah elephant before the inevitable last shot laid him out. An eight-foot tigress which was ringed near Dhoba on the first day charged two elephants after being wounded and was shot in the nick of time by Lieut.-Col. Harvey of the Prince's staff. Usually, however, the tiger was killed immediately he showed himself.

Rhinoceroses were much more difficult to track down. They could not be " ringed " like tiger, and when trailed through the jungle they moved with amazing swiftness. The Prince went out four days after big game, and two days to shoot jungle fowl. The only day in which the party remained in camp was Sunday, December 18, when the Prime Minister brought a very fine collection of wild animals, trapped in various parts of Nepal, as presents for the Prince. They were conveyed in rough cages, borne by stout little Nepalese, or led by ropes. and when the procession halted in front of the Prince's tent it resembled a circus on the march. A baby elephant headed the column. Then came a diminutive, very perplexed rhinoceros in a tight-fitting wooden prison. Followed two sambhars, goats, two bears, a leopard, a beautiful black panther baring its teeth viciously to all comers, musk deer, falcons, an iguana, a python behind heavy bars, partridges, jungle fowl, and two savage Thibetan mastiffs. The total bag for the week's shoot in Nepal was fourteen tigers, seven rhinoceroses, two leopards and two bears.

While in camp the Prince was entertained by a Gurkha brass band which played the latest popular airs, and by Nepalese dances given under the trees by the light of oil lamps. He received many curious and valuable gifts from the Maharaja including ivory and gold-mounted "kukris," embroidery and jade ornaments. The visit to Nepal ended on Wednesday evening, December 21, when his Royal Highness returned to Bikna Thori, *en route* to Patna and Calcutta.

The Royal train arrived at Paleza ghat on the Ganges at 9 o'clock next morning, and his Royal Highness proceeded down the river in the railway steamer *Benares* to Commissioner's Ghat, Patna. He drove in semi-state to the reception pavilion on the Maidan, escorted by Behar Light Horse, and received an address enclosed in a gold casket which was a model of a famous temple. Next day he met the feudatory chiefs of Orissa province at Government House; inspected the police and boy scouts, and walked through the lines of the 5th Northumberland Fusiliers and the Indian troops

Christmas week was spent in Calcutta. After a night's journey from Patna, the Prince was welcomed at Howrah station by the Governor of Bengal and high officials of the Presidency. His state barouche was escorted by the Viceroy's Bodyguard and an imposing array of infantry and cavalry to a pavilion in Dalhousie Square, where the Municipality presented its address. The Ruling Princes awaited him in the throne-room at Government House. That afternoon he was cheered by thousands of people on the famous race-course, when, after lunching with the stewards of the Turf Club, he witnessed the principal races of the day. On Christmas morning the Prince attended service at St. Paul's church, and visited the cruiser *Southampton* in the Hooghly, walking around the decorated mess decks. The remainder of the week was devoted to various public functions. He went again to the races on Tuesday, this time in semi-state, and drove slowly around the course before seeing the Viceroy's cup run. After the seventh race he presented the cup to Mr. Goculdas, whose horse "Roubaix" had won it. He attended a special Convocation of the Senate of the University, when the degree of Doctor of Laws was conferred on him.

He was up early one morning to take part in a paper chase. The same afternoon he drove to the Maidan and witnessed an open-air historical pageant provided by the Hindu and Mohammedan communities. A group of grave Hindu pundits in flowing robes came to him in a little open pavilion high above the crowd; offered rice, gold coins, blades of grass, and cocoanut, on gold plates as national emblems of fertility, and read an address in classical Sanskrit. Seven Mohammedan "Moulvies" followed with an address from the followers of the Prophet. Then one procession followed the other across the Maidan, passing in front of the pavilion and around the tiers of spectators. First was the Hindu pageant, a figurative representation of the seven principal notes in Hindu music, each of which has a caste, a colour and a presiding deity. Elaborately decorated platforms, drawn by bullocks, were occupied by the various gods and their attendants. Then came similar cars depicting the six principal Hindu seasons, each with its appropriate music, rendered by special instruments. The Mohammedan or " Nauroz " procession was an exact copy of that held by the Nawab Humayun Jah a century ago. It presented a confusing display of armed men in ancient costumes, and elephants and camels in rich trappings. Young girls in shimmering dresses of red and green silk, with transparent tinsel veils over their faces performed the sacred " Manipuri " dance in front of the pavilion. A company of some forty monks from a lamasery in Tibet, gave a grotesque lama dance, in which they wore huge " devil " masks and cumbersome ceremonial robes, and leaped about singly and in groups to the music of curious wind instruments. The spectators assembled around the open-air enclosure numbered many thousands, and the Prince had a very cordial reception when he drove around the edge of this dense throng, before the pageant began.

His Royal Highness' other engagements in Calcutta, included the opening of the new Victoria Memorial, which is intended to be a kind of Valhalla of the Indian Empire ; audiences with various Princes and ruling Chiefs, and a visit to the 2nd Royal Scots at Barrackpore. He saw the poor of Calcutta fed on the Maidan ; he unveiled the imposing war memorial, lunched at the Bengal, United Services and Calcutta clubs, and attended the customary dinner parties and dances at Government House, in addition to holding a levee at which more than 2,000 presentations were made.

The first phase of the Indian tour ended at Calcutta. On Friday afternoon, December 30, the Prince embarked at Outram Ghat in the Commissioners' steamer *Pansy*, and dropped down the Hoogly to Diamond Harbour, where the Royal Indian Marine troop ship *Dufferin* was waiting to carry him to Burma. By sunset he was steaming across the Bay of Bengal, and on Monday morning, January 2, Rangoon received him with open arms.

The Prince spent nine days in Burma. He regretted he could not stay much longer. From his arrival at Lewis street jetty, Rangoon, on the morning of January 2, until he sailed again for Madras, on the 10th, he was greeted everywhere by merry, smiling people, and there was not a single jarring note in the welcome that carried him on a wave of cheers to Mandalay and back. The cosmopolitan population of Rangoon proved their unity of purpose when they saluted him in the streets. Burmese, Armenians, Jews, Chinese, vied with each other in putting up elaborate stands and arches, known locally as "pandals" for the Prince's first drive from the harbour to Government House. A public holiday was proclaimed in his honour, and Rangoon did no work while he remained in the city. The Armenian Patriarch blessed him from the "pandal" of the assembled community; tiny Chinese children in coats of flowered silk, offered him flowers with shy little bows; dainty Burmese ladies clad in flaming petticoats and smoking black cheroots smiled at him from Ford cars. A bewildering mixture of the peoples of Asia gave the Prince his first welcome in cheerful Burma.

Ex-service men came from stations far upcountry to spend half an hour with him in Dalhousie park. Their delight at seeing him touched the Prince deeply. Many of them were old comrades from the battlefields of France who had abandoned everything at their country's call, and were now trying to rebuild their fortunes again in the jungle. The Prince walked and talked with them, and sat with them at tea under the trees. The same afternoon he visited Rangoon University where the boy and girl students were assembled in native costume. A Burmese ode was recited, and he saw an unusual game of ball played by expert students. Early next morning he reviewed the troops at a " proclamation parade," and a long day ended with a dance at the gymkhana club which had been transformed by coloured lamps and lanterns into a scene from fairyland.

The visit to Mandalay revealed another new aspect of the wonderful East. The Prince made the 18-hour journey in a light, almost toy-like train that swayed and jolted like a ship in a heavy sea as it travelled northwards. He found the " road to Mandalay " a pleasant road through a friendly country. He left Rangoon at 9.30 p.m. on January 4, with the lusty cheers of all classes of the community ringing in his ears, and was awakened before sunrise by voices singing in the wilderness. Dawn revealed the real Burma of tiny wooden villages set on stilts amid parched fields and the decayed remains of Buddhist shrines ; and country folk gazing at his saloon with twinkling eyes, and a smile instantly ready for the travellers. At every station he found the inhabitants awaiting him in a setting utterly unlike those prepared for his reception elsewhere. With the simplest materials they had evolved a gala dress far more effective than many costly and elaborate displays in other places. Palms and plantains, the symbols of peace and plenty, were the basis for a decorative background, with rows of plantains stuck in the freshly gravelled ground between rows of white painted wooden planks. Old petrol tins, disguised by a plain pattern of green and white (the colours used only to honour Royalty), had become artistic vases for flowers. Strips of clean matting were stuck fence-wise at intervals in the ground between taller plantains. In this modest very charming setting were the inhabitants of the district ranged on matting—rows of sedate men, women, boys, and girls, divided into groups according to sex and age, all dressed in their brightest colours, the little ladies displaying the " smart " pallor which is produced by a thick layer of rice powder, their hair carefully *coiffured* and glistening under their combs, all waiting in polite silence for the Prince. Behind the children sat the old village priest in his flowing yellow robes enthroned in a wooden chair, his hands folded in his lap, a benign smile on his wrinkled face. Thus every station on the road to Mandalay was like a section of a rainbow enclosed in a framework of Burmese boy scouts, and trimmed with flags and banners. No journey undertaken by his Royal Highness has been of greater interest or has revealed more sincere enthusiasm than this 400-mile trip through Burma.

When he reached his journey's end at 5 p.m. he was conducted to a great pavilion beside the railway station where the dignitaries of Upper Burma awaited him. Eight slant-eyed Shan Chiefs who had travelled many hundreds of miles with contingents from their tribes, had places of honour near the dais. Shan ladies of high rank, muffled in thick, hooded cloaks of padded silk watched wonderingly as the senior member of the Mandalay City Council, in a new bright pink skirt, intoned a long address in flowery Burmese. More than 4,000 men and women from the Shan States were placed along the Prince's route to the Fort, which lies within the old walls of the late King Theebaw's capital.

Although only two days were spent in Mandalay, this brief period was crowded with colour and incident. The evening entertainment arranged in his honour by the chiefs of the Northern and Southern Shan States easily ranked first in interest. The Shan peoples were encamped in a large enclosure outside the city walls. Each tribe had its own blocks of mat-roofed houses, and the temporary town which boasted of wide, regular streets and communal kitchens, adjoined a central square or village green, surrounded by the more ornate residences of the tribal chiefs, and by booths where embroidery, pottery, silverware, and other articles made by the Shans were displayed for sale. The Shans came in from the wilds with an amazing amount of luggage. They brought their historic gongs and bulky musical instruments, and all kinds of family heirlooms to show their importance in the eyes of the young Prince ; their best clothes and all their jewels, and as remarkable a collection of masks and pantomime costumes as has ever been seen outside Drury Lane. They had travelled for weeks by ox transport over the mountains and through jungle, some of them from the frontier of China, to give the Royal guest an evening's amusement.

There were black Shans from the region of the Mekong, where they feast on snakes ; Lus from the border of Chin ; Inthas from the Yawnghwe Lake, where they straddle their boats and paddle with their feet ; Karens, in gaiters, of black cord ; Was, who are head hunters and consequently looked down on socially by the Kachins ; and Kachins whose methods of courtship are gazed at askance by still more conservative tribes ; Zaycins, in short white shirts ; Palaungs, whose women have artificially lengthened necks held in place by brass tubing which varies from five to twenty-five coils according to the lady's age ; Hkuns, with massive turbans ; Taungthus, in red and black trousers and large spiked pins in their coarse hair ; and Bres in tight jackets and stone necklaces. There were Shan women with bobbed hair and women whose hair was worn coyly over the ears in early Victorian fashion, and women who hid their hair under tall hats of various coloured cloths. The dress parade of the Shan women showed conclusively that though fashions may come and go, there is nothing new under the sun.

The entertainment was given on the second evening of the Prince's stay. Six bearers, four of them the sons of chiefs, held golden umbrellas over him as he walked to a covered pavilion in the centre of the village "green." The chiefs did homage with much noise, and then began as strange a procession as the most feverish imagination could conceive. Out of the darkness appeared weird and monstrous animals, pirouetting forward to the rhythm of great gongs. There were fat dragons thirty feet long, and thin dragons twenty feet high; specimens of an unknown breed of emu with ten-foot necks; tigers with flaming jaws; and cats larger than any Dick Whittington ever dreamed of. Night-mare figures with the body, tail and feathers of a peacock, and dead-white faces—a mask suggesting some types of Buddha—gyrated back and forth and would not be stopped. It was like a menagerie of impossible beasts and birds suddenly gone mad with joy. The dragons chased their own tails and simulated drunkenness, and a pantomime ox with six legs proved its superiority over the conventional type in a race across the grass. Every tribe passed in review, during this grotesque parade, each in its own distinctive dress, and singing its own songs. Wild, painted warriors in high feathered head-dresses, brandishing bows and arrows gave way to long files of narrow-eyed, flat-cheeked women with shorn black locks, curtseying to the steady drone of gigantic pipes. The women with the giraffe-like necks passed with conscious pride, giggling shyly when they saw that their coils of silver tubing had attracted especial attention in the pavilion. The pandemonium was kept up indefinitely. Foolish dragons and friendly demons made their best bow, went away, came back again delighted, and indulged in more horse-play, first for the amusement of others, then for their own. Eventually they forgot they were performing for the Prince. Hours after he had gone away with deafened ears, the Shan pantomime still revolved across the green, stimulated furiously to fresh exertion by the gongs and drums. The tribes danced nearly the whole night through knowing they were a success and proud of it.

A crowded regatta on the moat adjoining the Fort gave the Burmese boatmen an opportunity of showing their skill in handling home-made racing craft. The banks were lined with spectators in flaming costumes, and groups of musicians with deep-sounding gongs were stationed at intervals to encourage the crews and stimulate the crowd. It was a lively, care-free assemblage. The little women chattered excitedly, and the men made bets with a knowing eye on the course. The Prince watched the races from a Royal barge built in the style of a " kalawait paung," a bird of good omen, that is said to have brought luck to one of the Kings of Burma. It was hung with gold paper, and furnished with tables and chairs, and looked, in fact, more like a floating temple than anything else. From an elevated seat the Prince had a clear view down the course—a straight stretch of waterway 150 yards wide and 440 yards long. Women as well as men competed in some of the twenty-three races, and the female crews drove their primitive shells—hollowed tree trunks—with remarkable skill and power. There were four boats from the state of Nyangwe, two rowed by men and two by women, and twenty-three boats from various districts of Upper Burma. The contests between the Burmese boats and those " manned " by the Intha women roused the native spectators to frenzy; they shouted and urged the competitors down the moat with fine enthusiasm. The

Intha women paddled with one foot, standing upright with other balanced on the shallow hull, and they won easily from the Burmese who wielded paddles in the orthodox style.

Native cart-races furnished another diversion for the Prince. The Burmese are born gamblers, and they flocked to a kind of Derby-day meeting outside the Fort with as keen interest in the events as is displayed by the pilgrims to Epsom. Cart-racing is one of their most popular forms of speculation. The carts—of light bamboo—are drawn by bullock teams, and only two teams can race at a time. The Burman studies " form " seriously. He could be seen inspecting the competing teams in the " paddock," as he thoughtfully puffed a green cheroot, and the principal bookmakers on the course, Mr. Poo and Mr. Ge Gen, were busy taking odds to the accompaniment of clashing cymbals and gongs. Even the bullocks seemed to feel the spirit of the occasion as they plunged heavily down the course, urged by their jockey-drivers with hideous cries and threats of punishment. Altogether it was a scene that for noise, colour and animation could scarcely be surpassed.

Before leaving Mandalay, the Prince saw some of the newest units of the Indian Army; regiments recently recruited in districts hitherto untouched by civilisation. They included Kachins and Chins, hillmen from the north-east and north-west frontiers respectively; military police mounted on diminutive ponies; pioneers and infantry representing areas where white men are rarely seen.

Rangoon gave the Prince a farewell spectacle which impressed him deeply. The Royal lakes in Dalhousie park were lit with prismatic fairy lamps and thousands of Chinese lanterns, and a procession of illuminated boats, led by the Royal barge, wound in and out of the little bays, while the sky blazed with fireworks. Next morning his Royal Highness drove through the massed population of the city to Lewis Street jetty, and re-embarked in the *Dufferin*. The river banks were black with cheering people ; tugs and small craft of all kinds followed in the *Dufferin's* wake until she had left the harbour far behind. The Prince stood on the bridge waving a regretful farewell, and the voice of Burma was last heard in a song from a passing launch : " Will ye no' come back again ? "

THE PRINCE GOING ON BOARD H.M.S. 'RENOWN' AT PORTSMOUTH, OCT. 26, 1921.

BIDDING GOOD-BYE TO HIS BROTHERS ON BOARD THE 'RENOWN.'

INSPECTING MARINES ON BOARD THE 'RENOWN' AT PORTSMOUTH.

THE PRINCE AND THE MIDSHIPMEN, H.M.S. 'RENOWN.'

H.M.S. 'RENOWN' LEAVING PORTSMOUTH.

MEMBERS OF THE PRINCE'S STAFF AT POGO EXERCISE.

THE PRINCE RECEIVING THE GOVERNOR OF ALGECIRAS AND HIS SUITE AT GIBRALTAR.

THE MOORISH CONSUL AT THE GARDEN PARTY AT GOVERNMENT HOUSE, GIBRALTAR.

H.M.S. 'IRON DUKE' ILLUMINATED IN THE GRAND HARBOUR, MALTA.

THE PRINCE ADDRESSING SCHOOL-CHILDREN ON ALAMEDA PARADE GROUND, GIBRALTAR.

NAVAL GUARD OF HONOUR AT CUSTOM HOUSE, MALTA.

MEETS RELATIVES OF MALTESE KILLED IN THE WAR.

AT A POLO GYMKHANA, MALTA.

THE PRINCE BEING WHEELED IN THE 'KING'S MESSENGER' RACE, MALTA.

THE 'RENOWN' PASSING THROUGH THE SUEZ CANAL.

INDIAN TROOPS ON THE BANK OF SUEZ CANAL CHEER THE PRINCE.

AEROPLANE ESCORT IN THE SUEZ CANAL.

ON HIS WAY TO THE TANKS, ADEN.

THE PRINCE IS PRESENTED WITH A SWORD FROM THE IMAM OF SANA, ADEN.

THE PRINCE REPLYING TO THE CITY'S ADDRESS OF WELCOME, IN THE AMPHITHEATRE, BOMBAY.

MEETING HIS INDIAN STAFF AND RULING PRINCES BEFORE LANDING AT BOMBAY.

MEETING LORD READING AT THE 'GATEWAY OF INDIA,' BOMBAY.

HEIRS APPARENT OF RULING PRINCES ON THEIR WAY TO PAY HOMAGE TO THE PRINCE AT GOVERNMENT HOUSE, BOMBAY.

WITH THE MAHARAJA OF KOLHAPUR, AND THE GOVERNOR OF BOMBAY, POONA.

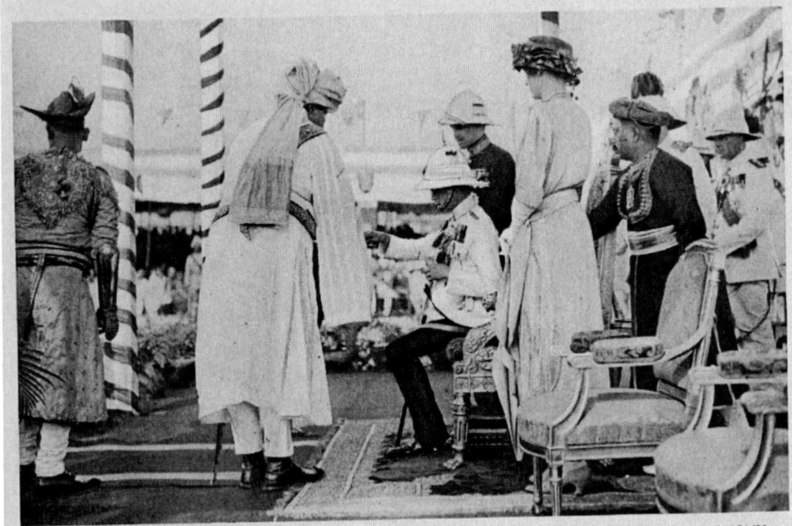

RECEIVING GIFTS FROM THE MAHARAJA OF KOLHAPUR, AT THE SHIVAJI MEMORIAL CEREMONY, POONA.

INSPECTING VETERANS OF THE INDIAN ARMY, POONA.

AMONGST THE CROWD AT POONA RACES.

THE GAEKWAR'S PERSONAL BODYGUARD, BARODA.

ARRIVAL AT LAXMI VILAS PALACE—THE PRINCE'S RESIDENCE DURING HIS STAY, BARODA.

WITH THE GAEKWAR OF BARODA AT LAXMI VILAS PALACE.

PRESENTATION OF COLOURS TO THE 1/7 RAJPUTS, BOMBAY.

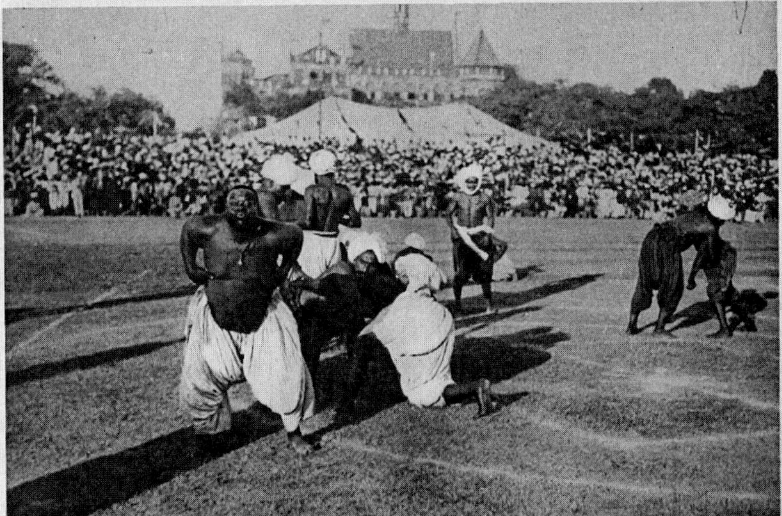

NATIVE WRESTLERS AT MILITARY TOURNAMENT, BOMBAY.

AT THE INSPECTION OF POLICE, BOMBAY

THE PRINCE SEES NATIVE SOLDIERS—MAIMED DURING THE WAR, BOMBAY.

E

THE GORGEOUSLY DECORATED ELEPHANTS WHICH TOOK PART IN THE CELEBRATIONS, BARODA.

ELEPHANTS AT THE GARDEN PARTY, BARODA.

WATCHING SIR LIONEL HALSEY STARTING ON AN ELEPHANT TRIP, BARODA.

THE STATE ARTILLERY'S BULLOCKS, BARODA.

ARRIVAL AT UDAIPUR STATION.

NATIVE GUARDS ON THE ROUTE TO THE RESIDENCY, UDAIPUR.

THE PRINCE AND THE MAHARAJA KUMAR AT THE RESIDENCY, UDAIPUR.

UDAIPUR'S METHOD OF ROAD WATERING.

NATIVE WARRIORS, JODHPUR.

THE PRINCE AND THE MAHARAJA REGENT, SIR PERTAB SINGH, JODHPUR.

WITH THE MAHARAJA OF JODHPUR.

PIG-STICKING AT JODHPUR.

THE PRINCE INSPECTING THE JODHPUR LANCERS—WHO WON FAME DURING THE LATE WAR, JODHPUR.

A PICTURESQUE GROUP AT BIKANER.

THE PRINCE WITH THE MAHARAJA OF BIKANER, INSPECTING THE CAMEL CORPS.

A SQUADRON OF THE CAMEL CORPS, BIKANER.

A NATIVE DANCING ON THE SHARPENED TEETH OF SAW BLADES, BIKANER.

HIS SON, A BOY OF THREE, DANCING ON SWORD BLADES.

THE PRINCE HITTING A GOAL ON THE POLO GROUND, BIKANER.

INDIAN DANCERS, BIKANER.

THE ROYAL BAROUCHE PASSING GAILY DECORATED SHOPS IN THE NATIVE QUARTER, BHARATPUR.

THE STATE LION WITNESSES THE PASSING OF THE PRINCE, BHARATPUR.

AT THE PENSIONERS' CAMP, LUCKNOW.

DISTRIBUTING FOOD AND BLANKETS TO THE POOR, LUCKNOW.

A VISIT TO KING GEORGE'S MEDICAL COLLEGE ACCOMPANIED BY THE VICE-CHANCELLOR OF THE UNIVERSITY OF LUCKNOW.

AT LUCKNOW RACES WHERE THE PRINCE RODE TWO WINNERS AND TWO SECONDS.

CONTRASTS IN TRANSPORT. THE MAHARAJA OF BHARATPUR'S CARRIAGE AND THE PRINCE'S CAR.

A NATIVE PRIEST WAITING TO BLESS THE PRINCE, BHARATPUR.

STATE CAVALRY ESCORT, BHARATPUR.

F

AT RAMNAGAR PALACE; THE PRINCE'S SUNSHADES.

THE PRINCE WEARING HIS GOWN AND AN ELABORATE GARLAND AFTER RECEIVING A DEGREE AT BENARES UNIVERSITY.

THE PRINCE LEAVING RAMNAGAR PALACE, BENARES, TO CROSS THE GANGES.

INSPECTING NEPALESE GUARD OF HONOUR WITH THE MAHARAJA OF NEPAL.

THE PRINCE'S FIRST TIGER, NEPAL.

IN THE JUNGLE, NEPAL.

WAITING FOR THE TIGER TO BREAK COVER, NEPAL.

THE PRINCE ON A 'PAD' ELEPHANT, NEPAL.

THE PRINCE ON A 'PAD' ELEPHANT, NEPAL.

ON THE WAY TO A TIGER SHOOT, NEPAL.

A MID-DAY HALT, NEPAL.

THE PRINCE WITH HIS HOST, THE MAHARAJA OF NEPAL.

THE MAHARAJA OF NEPAL PRESENTING AN OIL PAINTING OF HIMSELF TO THE PRINCE.

THE FRONTIER OF NEPAL.

THE PRINCE KICKS OFF, NEPAL.

GREETING MEMBERS OF THE RECEPTION COMMITTEE, PATNA.

INSPECTING THE GUARD OF HONOUR OF CALCUTTA SCOTTISH AT HOWRAH STATION, CALCUTTA.

ACKNOWLEDGING 'THREE CHEERS' AFTER PRESENTING CUPS AT THE RACES

MANIPURI DANCING GIRLS AT THE PAGEANT, CALCUTTA. MAIDAN

G

THE PRINCE ON THE ARAB PONY, A CHRISTMAS GIFT FROM HIS INDIAN STAFF, CALCUTTA.

THE VICTORIA MEMORIAL HALL, CALCUTTA.

AT THE UNIVERSITY COLLEGE, RANGOON, PRESENTATION OF A BURMESE ODE AND AN ADDRESS.

THE PRINCE'S ARRIVAL IN RANGOON.

BURMESE LADIES AWAITING THE PRINCE, RANGOON.

AT GOVERNMENT HOUSE GARDEN PARTY, RANGOON.

BURMESE LADY STUDENTS AT THE UNIVERSITY COLLEGE, RANGOON.

BURMESE LADIES.

THE PRINCE AND HIS UMBRELLA ESCORT AT MANDALAY.

BUDDHIST PRIESTS, MANDALAY.

SHAN TRIBAL DANCES. ONE OF THE THEATRICAL ANIMALS WHICH TOOK PART.

THE ROYAL BARGE 'KARAWEIK PAUNG' TOURING THE LAKE, RANGOON.

THE WELCOME AT MYSORE

INDIA

FROM MADRAS TO KARACHI

WHEN the Prince landed at Madras on the morning of January 13, he found himself in a different India. It was the India of the children's books: tall palms waving over flat fields, and the Dravedian people moving listlessly under a burning sun; a land of pallid Europeans in white clothes, and of punkahs struggling constantly against the damp, enervating heat. Madras looks like a bit of the East one visualized when reading "Little Henry and His Bearer." The rambling bungalows set in compounds like private parks, the interminable avenues and the general air of placid contentment contrast strangely with the bustling, wholly modern spirit of Calcutta and Bombay. Madras clings to the past. It is a distinct link with the opulent days of "John Company"—a city of fine character, mellowed by time, perhaps a little shabby and down at heel, but still prosperous and proud of its history. There are more English-speaking Indians in Madras than in any other city in India, and the Prince had a rousing welcome as he drove from the harbour to Government House over a route three and a half miles long. The children of fifty schools were gathered in stands in Esplanade road; thousands of Indian pensioners and ex-service men, many of whom had travelled long distances, stood in front of their camp near Government

House. The Prince found genuine enthusiasm everywhere he went. At no time did the organised outbreaks of discontent "non-co-operationist" touch his route.

He was four days in Madras. The people cheered him on the Guindy racecourse, when, on two occasions, he arrived in state to witness the principal events of this popular meeting. He strolled in front of the stands and through the crowd before the Prince of Wales' Cup was run, and the spectators pressed around him with shouts and clapping of hands. He was nearly mobbed by a horde of enthusiastic boy scouts and girl guides, to say nothing of smaller "blue birds" and "cubs," when he inspected those juvenile enthusiasts in the grounds of Government House. Fifteen thousand school children gave him another tumultuous reception on the banks of the river Cooum. He met 1,000 police at one parade and 2,000 pensioners at another. When his official engagements permitted, he played polo, and he also found time to visit some of the historic buildings.

The journey northwards, which took his Royal Highness through another series of important native States, began on the night of January 17, when he left Madras in an eruption of fireworks, attended to the railway station by thousands of people. Next morning he was in the cool, crisp atmosphere of Bangalore, the largest military station in Southern India, where he reviewed the garrison. The only British infantry on parade were the Auxiliary Forces, most of them men from the Kolar goldfields, fifty miles distant; the cavalry included the Queen's Bays and native squadrons. The parade that followed this march past touched the Prince deeply, for the marchers were old pensioners and ex-service men who hobbled in fours past his Royal Highness. One ancient, too feeble to keep up with the others, was brought forward for a few minutes' conversation with the Prince. He was overcome with emotion and limped away murmuring " God Bless David."

Mysore was the next stopping place. The Maharaja was waiting for him at the railway station the morning after leaving Bangalore, and in the streets of his Highness' well-kept capital—a city of " surpassing neatness and order "—were masses of friendly Indians,—old and young, afoot and sitting in garlanded stands, and surrounding gaudy triumphal arches. The Prince's return call on the Maharaja was made at a palace which is one of India's most beautiful buildings. Its treasures include a marvellous throne of gold, silver, and ivory, used by Tipoo Sultan, and discovered in a lumber room when the British forces stormed Seringapatam. The Prince visited the ruins of Seringapatam Fort on the River Cauvery next day, and lunched in the Daria Daulat, Tipoo Sultan's summer palace, a few miles distant. He was much interested in the curious wall paintings, executed by Indian artists at the command of the Sultan, which adorn the outer corridor of this pavilion. They represent battles between the Sultan's forces, and the British troops, and the uniforms of the period are depicted with astonishing accuracy.

The last three days of the visit to Mysore state were spent in a shooting camp at Karapur, forty-five miles from the capital, which was the base for expeditions after tiger, and for the "keddah" arranged by the Maharaja in honour of the Prince. A " keddah " is a " round-up " of wild elephant, and takes place at intervals of two or three years, usually in the presence of a distinguished guest. The preparations require many weeks, and involve the mobilisation of hundreds of Khurus, who are aborigines, inhabiting the jungle. The elephants must be first shepherded from the wilderness into a large compound, where they are permitted to roam about until the " round-up."

For the Prince's "keddah" twenty-eight elephants, including an enormous tusker, four cows with calves, and two young tuskers, were caught in the first drive, three months before he arrived in Mysore. They were bathing in the Kubani river when the Khurus surprised them with cries and the beating of wooden clappers, and the lighting of bonfires along one bank. The elephants fled from the fires and sought an entrance to the jungle on the other side, further up stream. They found one and disappeared in the belief that they were still free. But they had fallen into a trap. The jungle was no more than twelve acres in extent, and which ever way they turned they found a high wooden stockade save on the river side, where a broad ditch barred them from the water. Here they roamed about restlessly, splashing occasionally in a bathing pool fed by a pumping engine. Khurus camped along the river ditch, feeding fires at night, and making an infernal din in the day time, and the timid elephant folk kept well away from them.

Within the enclosure several grass-roofed platforms were built forty feet above the ground, on stout timber supports, strong enough to resist the charge of the herd. While this was being done the elephants were kept at the upper end of the compound. The Prince occupied one of these platforms well inside the stockade, and from his perch amid the trees he could see the furious struggles of the fugitives below him as they were finally herded towards captivity. When the Maharaja and all his guests were safely aloft, a line of tame elephants, called "koomkies," led by a bull known as "Judas," entered the enclosure, and gangs of beaters with bells and trumpets disposed themselves on either side of the herd which was browsing nervously in the furthest corner. Then, amid a great uproar, the wild elephants were manœuvred through the underbrush and among the trees towards a funnel-shaped opening at the other end of the compound. Several times they were nearly pinned at the entrance to this bottle neck, only to break away with furious trumpetings in the vain search for a quiet avenue of escape. Finally, the Khurus and the " koomkies "—the latter reviled unmistakably by their brethren of the jungle—drove the majority of the wild elephants to the desired spot and lit fires behind them. It looked as though all twenty-eight would be pressed into the funnel, but the big tusker led a charge and most of his followers bolted again through the blinding smoke. Remained only four young elephants. These dismayed victims found themselves pushed relentlessly by heavier " koomkies " down a steep, narrow alleyway which was the neck of the funnel, into a circular pen measuring about ten yards across. When they were safely inside with seven " koomkies " wedged around them, there was scarcely room for them to move. The walls of this pen were of timber, and from a platform around the top the Prince, the Maharaja, and their suites looked down on the final scene. A screened-off portion of the gallery concealed the Maharani and the ladies of the court.

Despite their struggles, the four wild elephants were roped fore and aft to the tame elephants. They bellowed with rage, and tried to lie down on the green boughs that covered the ground ; one of them cried bitterly. Finally they were prodded and pushed into semi-submission, and their warders hauled them to the river adjoining, where they were allowed to bathe and reflect on a future devoted to hard work. The remaining wild elephants were roped on subsequent days. After three to four months close confinement, shackled to trees, the prisoners of a " keddah " become docile. Then they are sold at auction.

The finest go to the stables of Indian Princes; the others find their way into a circus, or a labour corps.

The Prince left Mysore on the evening of January 23. His host lit up the capital magnificently, and the palace was outlined even to the cornices and pinnacles in incandescent lamps. All the inhabitants turned out to witness the farewell journey, and the Prince's last view of Mysore, as the Royal train passed into the night, was of an enchanted city gleaming like a great jewel against a background of black velvet.

Hyderabad, the largest and one of the wealthiest of the native States was reached after a hot, wearisome journey of two nights and a day. The ancient and picturesque capital offered the Prince yet another new aspect of Indian life. It lacks the tidy, well-swept appearance of Mysore, and the bazaars do not pretend to be as modern and well built as those of some other capitals, but they have a very distinctive character. Travellers often are reminded of Bagdad and Damascus by the narrow streets, with their whitewashed facades, and tiny shops raised above the traffic, and by the unusual number of Mohammedan women shrouded in shapeless hoods. Hyderabad is under a Mohammedan administration. Graceful minarets rise above the house tops, and many bearded teachers of the Koran are encountered in the bazaars. The ruler is the Nizam, premier prince of India, whose proudest title is "Faithful Ally of the British Government." He welcomed the Prince with impressive ceremonial and more than 100,000 of his subjects, including 14,000 school children, witnessed their 5-mile journey together from the railway station to Falak-numa palace. The crowd lay thickest around the low white shops and houses that line the straggling main street, and at the imposing Char-minar, a tall, square, tower-like building with four slender minarets, spanning the road on lofty archways. The route was framed in native infantry, and the Nizam turned out all his troops to make a fitting display of the resources of his State. At the palace on the hill the Prince found the Green Howards as his guard of honour.

The first morning was filled with heavy ceremonial, to the great delight of the population. Gorgeous processions passed and repassed through the winding high street between Falak-numa and Chowmahalla, the official residence of the Nizam, to the crash of field batteries and the music of military bands. The Nizam and his court awaited the Prince in a durbar hall, when his Royal Highness paid the usual return visit. African cavalry saluted him at the portals of the palace, and a string band played softly during the acts of homage. The state banquet in the evening showed Chowmahalla at its best. The fountain courts were flooded with light when the 200 guests were ushered into the state apartments, and the Nizam seemed determined to outdo all other Indian rulers in the profusion and originality of his electrical decorations. He sat at dinner beside the Prince, while from behind his chair, his two little daughters watched the scene with grave attention.

Next day the Prince reviewed 3,500 troops at Secunderabad, the British cantonment adjoining Hyderabad city. The march past included the 5th Cavalry Brigade, with the 4th Dragoon Guards, 5th Cavalry, Deccan Horse, and two regiments of Hyderabad Lancers. The infantry comprised the 2nd Bedfords, 1st Green Howards, and 75th Carnatic Infantry. They made a fine showing, and the Prince was struck by the soldierly bearing of the young recruits. The visit to Hyderabad lasted four days, and concluded with military sports at Secunderabad. The efforts of the Nizam's Government to make his stay enjoyable were shown by their completely returfing the Maidan at great expense, that he might have the finest possible polo ground.

Leaving Hyderabad on January 28, the Royal train travelled all that night and the next day through flat, uninteresting country dotted with little villages, and on the morning of the 30th arrived at Nagpur, the capital of the Central Provinces. The European community had worked for three months preparing for this one-day visit. They put up stands and arches—one arch composed entirely of orange trees with clusters of fruit attached—to make attractive his route to Government House. Sixteen ruling Chiefs of the Central Provinces were received by his Royal Highness at a Durbar in the grounds of the official residence, and Indian officers, pensioners and members of the Legislative Council were presented. Late that night, after a dinner party and a dance, the Prince resumed his journey. The next day was spent in travelling back to the main railway line, and another change of trains had to be made at Bhusaval junction, where the metre gauge line was taken to Indore.

The brief visit to Indore, one of the Central Indian states, comprised one event of outstanding interest, the Durbar at Daly College. The Maharaja Holkar escorted his Royal Highness to Manik Bagh palace, which had been placed at his disposal, and in the evening gave a banquet in his honour at Lal Bagh, a palace which shows the influence of Versailles. Eighteen ruling Princes and Chiefs of Central India were present at the Durbar, and the Prince made an effective little speech, and garlanded them. He motored from Indore to Mhow on the last day, and reviewed the troops. An unusual incident was the presence of the 11-year old daughter of the Maharaja of Dhar, who led her father's Light Horse past the saluting

THE PRINCE AT THE TAJ MAHAL

base. She wore service uniform and rode astride with great self-possession, rapping out the words of command in a shrill clear voice to the great delight of her father. The other troops on parade included the 60th Rifles, Outram Rifles, 22nd Punjabis, and 7th Hussars. The Prince joined the Royal train at Mhow and left at 6 p.m. for Bhopal.

A strange, veiled figure in a loose fitting, light blue robe, surrounded by Indian officials in black coats, awaited the Prince at Bhopal railway station next morning. As he stepped from his saloon, this mysterious personality came forward with outstretched hand, and in perfect English bade him welcome. It was the Begum, the only woman ruler in Asia. She administers the government of Bhopal with justice and wisdom, and, although her features are hidden from the world, she is, nevertheless, as active and as powerful as any Indian Prince. Through the shapeless veil that conceals her features she keeps keen watch on her Government. She is shrewd, kindly and discerning ; a loyal friend of Britain, and a close student of English history and literature. She follows the troubled course of Indian politics closely, yet finds time to teach her little grandchildren chapters from the Koran and to supervise their lessons. She even finds time to write books.

This interesting old lady was a perfect hostess. She took the Prince to the Royal barouche, chatting easily the while, and as they drove through the pleasant little capital to Lal Kothi, a white palace on a hill above a lake, she pointed out the various places of interest, and the curious accessories of his state reception. She showed him the official elephants, each bearing a "qur," the ancient Moghul symbol of sovereignty. They saluted with uplifted trunks while their mahouts, in gold livery, held metal emblems in the form of outstretched hands affixed to long poles, and others representing impossible dragons. Before Her Highness received the formal return visit of the Prince at Sadar Manzil palace, later in the morning, she personally supervised the arrangements for the ceremony, and walked around the Hall issuing directions in a quiet authoratative voice. She wore a belted robe of rich light blue brocade embroidered in purple, and a " burqa "—a long veil of cream lace draped from a flat, box-like cap that hid her hair. Across her forehead was a broad circlet of diamonds. She is short and inclined to stoutness, but she walks with great dignity; her voice is clear and pleasant, and those who know her say she has a merry laugh.

The visit was very impressive. The Prince and the Begum sat on silver thrones in the lofty marble and gilded hall, facing an open court flooded with brilliant sunlight. In a low balcony behind the dais were the little granddaughters of the Begum, in white, gazing on the ceremony with awe. Nobles and officials of the government in black frock coats were ranged on one side, and the staff of the Prince in white uniforms on the other. The lesser seats were covered with old tapestries, and silk carpets of many hues lay on the floor. The Begum talked in low conversational tones as her people came to the dais and were presented, indicating the first one with a wave of the hand and the words in English, " This is my eldest son." She made a long speech in Hindustani after the state banquet, the same evening, entering the hall when dinner was over, attended by one of her ladies, and taking her place beside the Prince. For two hours thereafter she chatted with the various guests, showing the liveliest interest in current topics, and frequently astonishing her hearers by her intimate knowledge of European affairs.

The three succeeding days of his stay in Bhopal State

were spent by the Prince in a shooting camp at Kachnaria, 22 miles from the capital, from which he made excursions after tiger, panther and sambhur. He returned in time for an American polo tournament at Bhopal on the afternoon of February 7, at which the Begum was present.

From Bhopal the Prince went to Gwalior State, which adjoins the Begum's territory on the north. He made his state entry in an elephant procession, that was one of the finest spectacles of the Indian tour. The Maharaja Scindia met the Royal train early in the morning, some miles from the capital, and at Gwalior station he ushered the Prince into a pageant such as his Royal Highness will hardly ever see again. Outside the station the Prince found the king of all elephants kneeling humbly in the dust—an enormous beast named " Hiragaj " said to be 100 years old, and surrounding him in a semi-circle eighteen other state elephants hardly less gorgeous. " Hiragaj " seemed of an incredible age, for the long heavy " whisk " of white yak's hair which his mahout held in front, drooped over his forehead and gave him the appearance of wearing an ill-fitting wig. He carried a gold two-seated howdah lashed to his back over a long mantle of dark crimson silk, his legs and body were plastered with gold paint, and he was hung about with tinkling bells. He surveyed the assemblage sadly through eyes newly rimmed with red paint—a strange contrast with the yellow ochre of his mournful face, and his feet supported massive silver anklets. He was altogether a weird and compelling sight. The Prince and the Maharaja reached the crest of "Hiragaj" by a long ladder, and amid a flourish of trumpets he stood upright and began his march. The other elephants followed in couples, bearing the sirdars of Gwalior and the members of the Prince's staff. Six elephants were silvered all over, and carried silver howdahs; the others were mostly light blue with gaudy side cloths, and cubist designs spread over their heads and trunks.

The procession wound through the streets and under the great gateway to the palace. In the vanguard were ordinary elephants carrying enormous kettle drums ; others with tall crimson standards supportea by Indian officers ; files of led horses in multi-coloured trappings, with handfuls of gay ribbons on their forelegs, and jewelled aigrettes behind their ears ; Gwalior cavalry ; guns ; foot soldiers staggering under the weight of more standards ; palanquins like small bungalows—one plated with gold and borne with difficulty by a company of palace attendants, and state carriages drawn by bullock teams. Mere words cannot convey an adequate impression of the barbaric splendour of the calvacade that led the way for " Hiragaj " and his proud companions. The Maharaja Scindia—one of the most enlightened and progressive of the rulers of Indian States—seemed determined to provide a setting for the Prince's reception that would outshine all other attempts to recall the ancient glories of India.

No less impressive was the scene of the Prince's formal return visit two hours later, when the Maharaja in pale mauve and belted with pearls worth a king's ransom was the central character in a well-staged ceremony. Singing women chanted a haunting Indian melody at the great door, as the offerings of betel and scent, and heavy garlands of gold thread were borne in procession by high officials through the throng of Mahratta chiefs to the dais.

In the afternoon the Prince saw the modern side of Gwalior. He opened the new King George Park which has been carved out of part of the gardens of Jai Bilas palace as a pleasure ground for the people of the city. The Maharaja has shown his broad-mindedness by erecting buildings for the various faiths of his people : a Hindu temple, a mosque, a house for the Theosophical Society, and a temple for the Sikhs. Eventually a Christian church will be added. There are sports' fields, a menagerie, and pavilions where the poor can purchase refreshments. The Prince unlocked the park gates with a gold key and spent an hour in the crowded enclosure, inspecting the buildings, and watching acrobatic feats and native sports. In the evening he was present at the state banquet, and next morning reviewed the Gwalior state forces. This parade was of exceptional interest, for the Maharaja wanted to show what his State could do in an emergency, and he turned out 5,000 troops of all arms, completely equipped for field service. Their smartness and efficiency evoked universal commendation. The Maharaja's two small children—George, the 6-year-old heir apparent, and Mary, who is a year older—marched as privates with the infantry battalion. They carried full kit and miniature rifles, and saluted the Prince with great gravity. The review concluded the official duties of the visit. Arrangements had been made for shooting expeditions on subsequent days which yielded good sport. Tigers were driven toward fixed positions, and eight were shot by the Royal party.

The Prince left Gwalior on February 12, and spent the next day at Agra. Early in the morning the Royal train stopped at Fatehpur Sikri, the ruined and deserted capital built by the Emperor Akbar. His Royal Highness wandered for two hours among the palace buildings and the great mosque, which even after three centuries appears to have been abandoned for only a few years. At Agra he paid two visits to the Taj Mahal, the last by moonlight; he inspected the ex-service men, and attended a garden party at the Fort which concluded with a torchlight tattoo by the K.O.S.B.'s. The Prince was to meet them again during his travels, for the battalion was transferred to

Egypt soon afterwards, and the officers and some of the men greeted his special train at Ismailia, on the way from Suez to Cairo, four months later.

The week of February 14-21, was spent in Delhi, the new capital of India. The official programme was heavy and exacting, but the Prince fulfilled all engagements with his usual energy and determination, and showed no signs of fatigue as he discharged the many duties imposed on him. He was received at Selimgarh Bastion station by the Viceroy and the principal members of the Government and high Indian personages, and drove in state through the Fort and the European quarter to Viceregal Lodge. His route was roughly three and a half miles long, and it is estimated that 60,000 natives were assembled along it, including detachments of the "depressed" classes, and many delegations from the surrounding towns and villages which had been brought in by special trains.

The first important ceremony of the week was the unveiling of the All-India Memorial to King Edward, a fine equestrian statue by Brock, which has been erected on a commanding site in the Memorial Gardens. It cost 5 lakhs of rupees, and represents the offerings of 80,000 persons of all sections of the community from all parts of the vast continent of India. Next day His Royal Highness went to New Delhi—a wilderness of unfinished public buildings and newly created avenues six miles from the present city—and laid the foundation stone of the Kitchener College. This institution, in the words of the Viceroy, will form an avenue of entry into an Indian Sandhurst, so that the sons of Indian officers may attain to full executive rank of the Indian Army. Representatives of all the units in the Indian Army marched past the Prince after the ceremony. He was again in touch with the Army on the following afternoon at a Garden Party given by native officers in the Fort. The ruling Prince's banquet to his Royal Highness at Maiden's hotel, brought together nearly all the great overlords of the native states, and even the Begum of Bhopal was in the distinguished assemblage that listened to the brief after-dinner speeches. The State banquet at Viceregal Lodge was the most brilliant function of the kind held in Delhi for many years. There were nearly 250 guests, including Indian Princes, all the high British and Indian officials of the Empire, and officers of the army and navy.

The Prince made his first speech in Urdu, when he presented colours to the 16th Rajputs on the polo ground on Sunday, February 19, after a military parade service. He spoke in simple sentences, with an excellent accent, and the native troops were surprised and very pleased. A detachment of Indian police was inspected on Monday, in the grounds of Viceregal Lodge. The same afternoon his Royal Highness witnessed one of the most exciting games of polo ever played in Delhi. The competing teams, representing Jodhpur and Patiala, are famous throughout India. Sir Pratap Singh watched the fortunes of Jodhpur with tense face, and when his people gained the victory the old man nearly collapsed with joy. The Prince played polo himself, watched by a large crowd, on several afternoons during his stay in Delhi.

Three days were spent at Patiala, on the way to Lahore, the first day occupied with the usual formal functions, and the remainder being devoted to polo and pigsticking.

From Patiala, the Prince journeyed overnight to Jullundur, where he laid the foundation stone of the first of the King George's Military schools, which are to be used as boarding schools for the sons of Indian soldiers. He was met by pensioners representing every arm of the service, and every campaign in which Indian troops have participated since 1857, and by 2,000 school children.

At Lahore, the Prince was in the country of the Sikhs. Special trains brought the farmers and villagers from many places in the Western Punjab to see him drive to Government House on the afternoon of February 25. A great provincial fair, or "mela," which was much like provincial fairs the world over, drew thousands of excursionists to the outskirts of Lahore during the Royal visit. Here the Prince and the people met under unusual circumstances, when he witnessed an entertainment organised in his honour, and the Sunday afternoon he spent with these people of the provinces was, without doubt, the most unusual experience of his stay in Lahore. He was met at the entrance to the fair ground by local sirdars of the Punjab in gold coats, and by 250 of their mounted retainers brandishing lances ornamented with fluttering ribbons. This escort took him through the dense throng of Indians and around the sports amphitheatre to his balcony on the grandstand. The crowd was interested and wholly good humoured, and there were many shouts of welcome as the Prince rode at the head of this column of horsemen across the Maidan. He saw a musical ride by Patiala Lancers, and amusing feats by acrobats and jugglers. The "mela" was an instructive as well as entertaining exhibition, and in addition to the usual side-shows for the simple peasantry, there were exhibits of agricultural machinery and improvements for their farms, and specimens of the handiwork of Punjabi craftsmen.

On another day the Prince visited the workshops of the North-Western railway at Moghulpura, near Lahore, where the Royal train was built, and walked through the shops where he saw the various stages of carriage construction. He met the members of the Punjab Legislative

AN IMPRESSION OF THE KHYBER PASS

Council in the Assembly Hall, and received an address of welcome; he rode with the Lahore hounds; attended a party in Shalamar gardens, and played polo when the opportunity offered.

The Prince's 27-hour visit to the Maharaja of Kashmir and Jammu, again showed the desire of the Indian rulers to entertain him regardless of expense. The preparations for his reception were on a scale calculated to stagger an ordinary European. He was to have been housed in the picturesque capital of Jammu, but plague broke out in the city two months before his arrival, and half-finished buildings had to be abandoned. A city of tents sprang up on the plain of Satwari, four miles from the "forbidden" city, and within a few weeks this camp was complete even to modern sanitation, electric lighting, telephones, and paved roadways ornamented with beds of flowers. A lofty building of brick had been erected as a banqueting hall, but the Maharaja did not like it, and at the last moment it, too, was "scrapped," and two spacious tents, lined with silk carpets, were thrown together as a drawing-room and a dining room for his guests. All the members of the court and the officials of Kashmir came down by road to join the retinue from Jammu on the plain. There came also merchants of Srinagar city, transporting their carpets and precious wares over the mountains to lay them before the Prince and his suite. They brought old silver and devil charms from Tibet; necklaces of jade; pottery; and papier mâché work; gold and silver vessels; raw turquoises; and century-old shawls—all this for a single day's display in the little market put up for them by the Maharaja. A company of Tibetan monks was brought from their lamasery at Hami, 400 miles from Jammu, especially to perform a lama dance. They started on their journey in October, before the passes were blocked by snow, hauling their curious masks and gongs in little carts.

The Maharaja built his own camp a mile from the temporary city of Satwari. He put up a durbar tent hung with £15,000 worth of old shawls, the roof was supported on pillars of inlaid silver, and on the low canopied dais at one end were two low silver thrones with arm rests of gold in the form of crouching lions. The Prince's apartments were in a plain modern building not unlike a French château, standing in a wooded park adjoining the tents of Satwari. It was furnished with the same lavishness. The carved wood furniture in his study—used by him less than two days—was made especially for him by the best craftsmen in Srinagar, who worked on it for a year. Everywhere were priceless shawls, all family treasures. The riches of Kashmir and Jammu were laid freely at the feet of the Royal traveller, and all the state elephants from Srinigar were on parade when he drove into Satwari camp. After the banquet on the evening of his arrival there were fireworks and the lama dance, and he rode back to his château on the biggest elephant. The Maharaja's troops were reviewed next morning—infantry, cavalry, and guns, all very fit and soldierly. The Prince left Satwari just before noon on the second day, and a little time afterward the caravans began the long journey back through the passes to Srinagar.

The last stage of the Prince's tour northward was from Satwari to Peshawar. He stopped twice in the afternoon after saying farewell to the Maharaja of Kashmir and Jammu; first at Sialkot where the 2nd Indian Cavalry Brigade, under Colonel Commandant Rankin, was waiting to be inspected; and then at Jhelum, at sunset, where he walked among a large gathering of Indian pensioners and ex-service men from all parts of the district. Next morning he awoke in the keen, clear atmosphere of the North-West Frontier Province, and had his first view of the fighting men from the hills as they stood on the railway platform at Peshawar, wrapped in their heavy "poshtins."

Peshawar is one of the most interesting cities in India. Architecturally it makes no pretension to beauty; the bazaars are of the ordinary type found in other places, but they contain strange and varied elements of humanity, drawn across the frontier in the caravan traffic that passes twice weekly through the Khyber. Representatives of all the races of Central Asia can be seen between the Kabuli Gate and the Bajauri Gate. Afridis, Mohmands, and other border people predominate in the crowded streets, and there are also Afghans from Kabul; merchants from Samarcand and Merv; narrow-eyed Mongolians from the frontier of China; dealers in rugs from Bokhara; and Jews from Herat. The city sits in a plain, hemmed about by rocky heights, and the people within its walls know more of fighting and sudden death than those living in more secure, less picturesque, surroundings further south. Barbed wire entanglements protect the suburbs from night raids, and the traveller from the south is reminded of a town in war-time that has been brought uncomfortably close to the front line.

The day after his arrival, the Prince motored through the Khyber Pass to the Afghan frontier. He left Peshawar after attending service at St. John's church, and drove across the plain to Jamrud Fort, which guards the southern exit of the gorge. It was a beautiful bright morning, with the sun shining from a sky of deepest blue, but a piercing wind swept down the narrow valley which made the heaviest garments seem none too warm. Unfortunately the Prince did not see the Pass on a caravan day. It was clear of traffic and manned by the frontier garrisons that keep constant vigil on the twin roads leading into Afghanistan. All the hilltop forts and watchtowers, and the ragged crests that rise steeply on either side of the winding valley, were filled with riflemen. The rocky slopes looked bare and lifeless as he looked ahead from his car, but whenever he glanced back he found them teeming with soldiers. They stood at the salute in little groups on slender crags, and gazed down from dizzy heights at other frontier levies dotted along the road. More than 1,500 Afridi warriors, many of them ex-soldiers of the disbanded Khyber Rifles, were posted in and around the 23-mile long defile between India and the new frontier of Afghanistan in addition to the regular garrisons. These lonely outposts of the Empire made a brave attempt to be festive, but their meagre splashes of colour and fluttering flags merely emphasised the grimness and bleakness of the Pass. Messages of welcome had been laboriously picked out in whitewashed stones beside some of the little blockhouses poised among the clouds, their characters scarcely legible to the travellers in the gorge. At one turn in the road the Prince came suddenly on the 18th Mule Corps encamped in a barren pocket between the towering cliffs of Ali Musjid, their greeting emblazoned in 10-foot letters on the slope above their tents. All the military inhabitants of the Pass looked their smartest; even some of the walled-in mud settlements hung out bits of bunting. Shaggy Afridis from mountain villages squatted for hours beside the road near Landi Kotal to see the Prince pass, and showed the liveliest curiosity in his personality.

He spent two hours in the fortress of Landi Kotal where the 2nd Warwicks are stationed; he walked in trim barrack streets bearing familiar London names; inspected the men of the 1st Infantry Brigade, and lunched with the Colonel Commandant. He continued his journey over the rocky height of Michni Kandao, dropping 3,000 feet to the last British outpost at Landi Khana, where a detachment of Gurkhas look across a little valley into the Ameer's country. On the way back to Peshawar he stopped at Sarkai Shigr, near Jamrud Fort, to meet representatives of the entire Afridi nation. Nearly a thousand " maliks," or village elders, mostly greybearded warriors, were crouching on carpets in the sunshine, around the chairs where the Prince sat with the Chief Commissioner of the North-West Frontier Province. The " maliks " presented him with fat sheep, ancient Afridi arms, and a specimen of the best modern rifle they can manufacture in their primitive arms factory across the border.

Next day the Prince drove in state through the native city of Peshawar. He was met at the Kabuli Gate by Afridi horsemen in chain armour, and escorted through the Qissa Khani—the Street of the Story Tellers—and the Coppersmith's Bazaar to the large central square known as the Hastings Memorial where an address was presented. A general " hartal," or day of mourning, had been declared by the shopkeepers as a protest against the arrest the night before of certain political malcontents. The shops, in consequence, were shut. This so angered the loyal chiefs from the hills that a deputation went to Sir John Maffey, the Chief Commissioner, and asked permission to deal summarily with the authors of this outrage on hospitality. Their spokesman craved permission for 5,000 hillmen to "re-open" the bazaars permanently—by taking off the roofs. The "maliks" consented reluctantly to keep the peace, but declared that the incident would not be forgotten.

Before leaving Peshawar on March 7, the Prince inspected detachments of the frontier forces, militia, constabulary, and police ; then the Peshawar garrison, and a large number of wounded and disabled ex-soldiers, as well as 3,000 able-bodied men who had come in from the border villages.

March 8 was spent in the Malakand, and here again he had an instructive insight into the routine of frontier life. At Chakdara, he met the Dirs and Swats, the opposing forces in a curious little war. These rival tribes fight annually until it is time to harvest the crops, but a truce had been declared for the Royal visit, and the combatants came in blithely to fraternise on the neutral ground of Chakdara Fort. When the Prince had gone they returned to the "theatre of operations," and the British outpost—rather in the position of spectators in the stalls—resumed surveillance of the sniping across open fields. Both sides sent their wounded to the fort.

During his last weeks in India the Prince saw a good deal of the Army. After visiting the Malakand, he reviewed the garrison at Nowshera. It was the largest parade he had yet witnessed, and included the 1st Indian Cavalry Brigade (with the 18th Hussars), the 4th Infantry Brigade (including the 2nd Lancashire Fusiliers), and a brigade each of field and pack artillery, with Air Force units and two Mule Corps. After the review the Prince motored to Taxila, where he inspected the wonderful Buddhist remains excavated under the supervision of Sir John Marshall. Continuing his journey in the afternoon he passed across the open country used for military manœuvres and early in the evening arrived at Rawal Pindi, where he was lodged at the Circuit House as the guest of Lord Rawlinson, the Commander-in-Chief.

The manœuvres which were to have taken place on a grand scale during his stay at Rawal Pindi were abandoned on account of expense. Instead, the Prince held a review of the troops, which numbered more than 10,000 of all arms, including the 2nd Connaught Rangers which appeared in a ceremonial parade for the last time before being disbanded. One incident of his stay which appealed particularly to the Indian troops was his meeting with Sepoy Ishar Singh, the first Sikh to win the Victoria Cross, which the Prince pinned on his tunic in the presence of his comrades.

Kapurthala was the last native State visited by his Royal Highness. He spent March 12 there as the guest of the Maharaja, arriving in time for lunch, and leaving after the State banquet. He stopped next day at Dehra Dun to open the Prince of Wales' Royal Indian Military College, and to present colours to the Sanawar Royal Military School. In the evening he arrived at Kadir Cup camp, near Gajraula, as the guest of Sir Harcourt Butler, Governor of the United Provinces, to see the Kadir cup, the blue ribbon of pig sticking. His Royal Highness left camp early next morning and watched various beats of the Kadir meeting, riding most of the time with the umpire. He saw the semi-finals and final of the Kadir cup on the morning of the 15th, and in the afternoon he competed in the Hog Hunter's (Light Weight) cup, in which His Royal Highness finished first on "Bombay Duck," the property of Captain West, R.H.A.

The Royal train left Gajraula on March 15, and after a dreary journey across the Sind desert, arrived at Karachi on the morning of the 17th. The Prince's last public function in India was the unveiling of the Baluch War Memorial. In the afternoon he said farewell to his Indian staff, and at 5 o'clock he drove from Government House through cheering crowds to the harbour. An hour later the *Renown* was under way for the Far East.

CEYLON TO HONG-KONG

A VOYAGE of three and a half days in pleasant weather brought the *Renown* to Colombo early on Tuesday, March 21. The Prince found himself in a land wholly friendly and loyal. The people of Ceylon waited hours in the sun to see him for five minutes; wherever he went he was surrounded by admiring natives. Their simple kindliness and frank devotion made a far deeper impression than mere pageantry. His first drive through the streets of Colombo was accomplished in an open motor car without escort of any kind, and the informality of this five mile journey up and down the shaded avenues, past bungalows and mansions filled with applauding spectators, was a welcome change from the set processions of the Indian tour. It was like an informal ride across London. One striking feature was passage through a triumphal avenue at the Chalmers rice granaries where 7,000 native workers sat in stands, and a band of drummers ushered him down the processional way with a wild tattoo. In the evening, the illuminated streets were overflowing with exuberant merry-makers afoot and in beflagged motor cars and jinrikishas. They blew tin trumpets, threw confetti, and made the night joyful while the Prince dined and danced at Government House. Colombo had not celebrated on such a scale for years.

The presentation of colours to the Ceylon Light Infantry next morning brought his Royal Highness in touch with many ex-service men. They saluted him in the barrack square of the old Fort : nearly a thousand veterans of all colours, castes, and creeds, who had served in the Sanitary Corps and other units in Mesopotamia, and facing them, other ex-soldiers in a strange variety of uniforms—men in police kit ; men in white drill ; men in Highland kilts ; men in worn khaki. After the presentation of the colours the Prince shook hands with every man. It was no light ordeal, with the noonday sun beating down on the shadeless square, but he went through it with a smile for each soldier, and no act could have appealed more strongly to them or to the spectators.

The Prince went to Kandy on Thursday morning, travelling in a special train that reached the ancient capital of the Kandyan kings just after noon. The three and a half hour's journey through one of the most picturesque portions of the island gave him ample proof of his popularity with the country folk. Every station from Colombo to Kandy was packed with people in holiday dress ; every little grass hut at the edge of the jungle showed some bit of decoration, if only a spray of cocoanut palm or a diminutive Union Jack, to emphasise the loyalty of the occupants. There seemed to be continuous lines of women, children, and village elders along the permanent way between the capital and Rambukkana, and the constant cheering drowned the rattle of the train. From Rambukkana the line climbs abruptly around the sides of precipitous hills, but even on those dizzy slopes were knots of smiling Cingalese, merging into a greater throng at the journey's end.

Kandy was overrun with people from the hills for miles round about. They poured into the town by special trains, and for many of them this meeting with the Prince was the event of a lifetime. The planters had come from their tea and rubber estates, and they furnished a guard of

, every man of which had seen active service. The streets and open places were congested with wondering sightseers ; it was a vast picnic for the native farmers and their families who were encamped on the grass near the lake.

A Durbar, at which the Prince met eighty Kandyan chiefs, the representatives of five districts, was held in the evening. It recalled the splendour of the Royal court that was at one time all-powerful in the hills. The chiefs were assembled in the old Hall of Justice, an open structure supported by massive pillars of carved wood. They wore the ceremonial dress of their rank—voluminous silk wrappings resembling padded skirts, ankle length white trousers with wide starched frills at the bottom, and hats of heavy silk brocade that looked like miniature pagodas. One young chief displayed three service ribbons on his tunic, and the Prince stopped to talk with him after the ceremony of homage which was performed in couples before the dais. After the Durbar the Prince was taken by a covered way to the famous Temple of the Tooth, one of the most sacred Buddhist shrines in the world, where a tooth, reputed to be that of the great teacher, is carefully preserved. He walked through a dimly lighted hall where monks and novices in saffron robes stood silent in the shadows, and into a smaller room enclosed in heavy steel bars which was the holy of holies. A reliquary, like a slender gold bell, nearly 10 feet high, was opened by the principal priest, and six caskets, one inside the other, were unlocked, until the innermost—a box studded with precious stones—was released. It was reverently removed and placed on a table; the lid was lifted, and the Tooth lay revealed by the flickering light of an oil lamp. Whatever the origin of the relic, it cannot by any stretch of the imagination be regarded as the tooth of a human being. For one thing it is much too large. Nevertheless, it has been for centuries the most precious possession of the Buddhist community in Ceylon, and pilgrims come in thousands every year to worship at the shrine.

After the exposition of the Tooth, the Prince was taken to the Octagon, a pavilion facing the Esplanade, where the Kings of Kandy received the homage of their subjects, and here he looked down on a wonderful religious procession, called the "perahera." Relics from the five principal Buddhist temples in the Kandy district were carried in miniature gilt temples lashed to the backs of temple elephants, escorted by other elephants—150 in all—and by delegations of priests and dancing men from the various centres of worship. A relic from the Temple of the Tooth, but slightly less precious than the Tooth itself, had the place of honour. It was borne solemnly under a canopy by a group of priests from its shrine in the temple to the "Tooth" elephant at the entrance. This gigantic beast, which was wrapped in a long cloth-of-gold mantle, is especially trained for its part in the "perahera," and it moved off solemnly at the head of the column, covered by a canopy carried on poles by twelve men. Each delegation was led by its "relic" elephant, and the temple dancers who leaped and writhed furiously to the music of native drums. They paused in turn before the Prince and tried to excel all the other contingents in the variety and vigour of their antics.

The Prince returned to Colombo on Friday in time to attend a race-meeting in the afternoon. He said farewell to Ceylon next morning, and at 11 o'clock the *Renown*, steaming 21 knots, left for Malaya. The third evening at sea he witnessed an amusing musical revue "The Cruise of the Ditty Box," in the forecastle theatre. The majority of the ship's company was present at this performance, for which special music and scenery had been prepared.

The Federated Malay States welcomed the Prince on Tuesday, March 28. The *Renown* anchored off the entrance to the new harbour at Port Swettenham early in the afternoon, and two hours later his Royal Highness was met at the jetty by the High Commissioner (who is also Governor of the Straits Settlements), and by the native rulers. A procession of princes in motor cars escorted him from Port Swettenham to Kuala Lumpur, the capital, 20 miles from the coast. The Sultan of Perak rode with the Prince, and he was followed by the Sultan of Selangor, the Yang di per Tuan of Negri Sembilan, and the Sultan of Pahang, all in gala robes. Kuala Lumpur is a cheerful, well-built town with fine driveways, modern public buildings, and a mixed native population in which the Chinese predominate. The shops and streets were lavishly decorated, as was the road from Port Swettenham, and the Prince was heartily cheered along the entire route. A Chinese torchlight procession organised in his honour passed the Selangor Club in the evening, and the dancing in the ballroom was stopped that his Royal Highness might see the quaint crawling dragons, the triumphal cars adorned by smiling Chinese maidens, and the companies of children carrying lighted lanterns. A public reception next morning brought many dignitaries of the Federated States before him in a pavilion facing one of the public squares, and surrounded by 1,400 school children and the majority of the adult population. Afterwards, at Government House, he invested the Sultan of Pahang with the insignia of an honorary K.C.M.G. A state ball at the town hall, a luncheon next day by the reception committee representing all nationalities, and an afternoon at polo completed the programme. His Royal Highness returned by train to Port Swettenham on Thursday afternoon, and *Renown* sailed that evening for Singapore.

CEYLON TO HONG-KONG

The two-day programme at Singapore kept the Prince fully occupied from the moment he landed at Johnston's Pier on Friday morning. The drive through the streets from the water front to Government House gave him a wonderful picture of the composite population of the busy port. Malays, Chinese, Indians, and Japanese were hardly less industrious than his own countrymen in helping dress the route in gay colours, and in adorning it with arches of original design. In a great amphitheatre built for the occasion were assembled 10,000 children of many nationalities, and the Prince made them happy by walking around the tiers of seats and listening to their singing. He unveiled an imposing War Memorial on the Harbour front. In the grounds of Government House he found 400 wild warriors from Borneo—Dyaks, Kayans, and other tribesmen—lightly clad in jackets covered with fishskin, and ornamented with strange necklaces of bones, shells, stones, tiger-cat teeth, and silver coins. As the Prince passed they brandished their spears and gave loud cries of welcome. The women were shy but interested, and one plucked up sufficient courage to show the Prince her arm which was sore and swollen from the effects of vaccination, as a protest against an inexplicable "punishment." The Prince saw the warriors again in the afternoon when he opened the Malaya-Borneo exhibition. A replica of a Dyak village had been erected on stilts in the exhibition grounds, and fitted with the rude furniture and household implements of these primitive people. They had even brought clusters of human skulls—the trophies of head hunting expeditions undertaken by their forefathers—and suspended them like chandeliers from the grass thatched roof of the long common room. Nothing pleased the men of Borneo more than for a visitor to examine these gruesome heirlooms and ask questions about their family feuds.

The Malaya-Borneo exhibition was an instructive and very complete display of arts and crafts of the native states. It covered many acres and comprised collections of silverware, wood carving, metal work, embroidery, specimens of native costumes, weapons and musical instruments, and elaborate models showing mining operations and the working of various industries. From the exhibition the Prince went to the Yacht club pavilion where he witnessed sea sports. On Saturday he informally inspected the 2nd battalion of the Middlesex regiment (the " Die Hards "), of which he is colonel-in-chief, at Tanglin barracks; met the ex-service men; lunched with the leading men of Singapore at the town hall, and visited the races. After dinner at Government House, he saw an exhibition of Dyak dancing. The warriors were massed on the lawn, and after a chant of welcome by the headmen, and a symbolic dance, his Royal Highness was presented with the complete costume and head-dress of a chief. A dance at the Town Hall, and another Chinese torchlight procession, were the two final events of the visit. After the dance, the Prince went on board the *Renown*, and she sailed early on Sunday morning for Hong-Kong.

Fog lay thick over Hong-Kong when the *Renown* arrived off the harbour on the morning of April 6, and for the first time during the tour the Prince's arrival was delayed. The mist lifted within an hour, and the battle cruiser passed to her anchorage amid the hooting of syrens, the explosion of thousands of firecrackers, and the salutes of British and foreign warships, including a Japanese squadron of light cruisers sent to act as escort on the voyage to Yokohama. British bluejackets lined the route from Blake's pier to a reception hall erected especially for the visit, and the Prince accomplished this short journey in a palanquin carried by eight Chinese bearers in white and scarlet costumes, his staff following on foot. At the hall he heard an address in flowery Chinese, which was read in the presence of British and Chinese officials, foreign consuls and representatives of the commercial community, and he then continued his journey in the palanquin up the steep hillside to Government House. In the evening he came "down town" again to see the illuminations which were very beautiful. All the principal buildings were lit uniformly by red Chinese lanterns, and the warships in harbour were outlined in lights. It was a matter of general regret that the whole of Hong-Kong's night display could not be seen. Mist enveloped the upper half of the "Peak,"—the high hill behind the city—and the very elaborate illuminations prepared on the upper slope and crest were hidden during the Royal visit.

On the second day of his stay his Royal Highness met the children from 42 schools; boy scouts and girl guides; inspected the 102nd Grenadiers (Indian Army); received an honorary degree from the University, and an address from the Masons. He made a happy impression when asked to permit the erection of a statue of himself in Statue Square, by replying that he preferred instead "that some very good thing be done for the community of Hong-Kong in his name." In the afternoon he attended the races at Happy Valley, a famous resort for all classes of the community, and saw the Prince of Wales' stakes run in the presence of an enormous crowd. The Chinese gave him a banquet of weird and costly dishes, in the auditorium of their principal theatre. The menu included such curious delicacies as shark's fin, "gold and silver eggs," and bird's nest soup. During the courses a company of actors from Canton performed an amusing little drama.

The Prince liked Hong-Kong, and before the *Renown* sailed next morning he was ashore early at Kowloon, visiting the markets and buying souvenirs in the shops. At 9 o'clock the Japanese cruiser escort led the way into the China Sea, and the people on the water front had a last glimpse of his Royal Highness saluting from his platform above the bridge.

The voyage to Japan took four days. Heavy weather was experienced in the Strait of Formosa, but thereafter the sea was smooth, and at 8 o'clock on Wednesday morning, April 12, the *Renown* was shown into Yokohama harbour where the 1st battle squadron and 1st battle cruiser squadron of the Japanese Fleet greeted the Prince with full ceremonial.

PRINCE PLAYING POLO AT MANDALAY.

BURMESE BOAT RACES, MANDALAY.

THE ROYAL BARGE ON THE MOAT, MANDALAY

THE PRINCE, SURROUNDED BY GIRL GUIDES, IN A SEA OF SOLAR TOPEES, MADRAS.

THE PRINCE MET BY THE GOVERNOR OF MADRAS.

AN EARLY MORNING RIDE ON THE ISLAND, MADRAS.

THE PRINCE GREETS INDIAN EX-SERVICE MEN, MADRAS

PLAYING POLO, MADRAS.

RIDING BETWEEN LINES OF SALUTING INDIAN PENSIONERS, BANGALORE.

THE PRINCE'S ARRIVAL, MYSORE.

THE COURTYARD OF THE PALACE, MYSORE.

THE MAHARAJA'S PALACE AT NIGHT.

THE PRINCE AND THE MAHARAJA AT THE TIGER SHOOT, MYSORE.

THE KEDDAH (WILD ELEPHANT HUNT). THE PRINCE SCALING THE STOCKADE.

THE PRINCE ARRIVING ON THE POLO GROUND, HYDERABAD.

PICTURESQUE RETAINERS OF THE MAHARAJA HOLKAR, INDORE.

THE NAWAB BEGUM OF BHOPAL SHAKING HANDS WITH THE PRINCE.

THE PRINCE AND THE NAWAB BEGUM OF BHOPAL PROCEEDING TO THE DURBAR HALL AT SADAR MANZIL PALACE.

LEAVING THE RAILWAY STATION, BHOPAL, WITH THE NAWAB BEGUM.

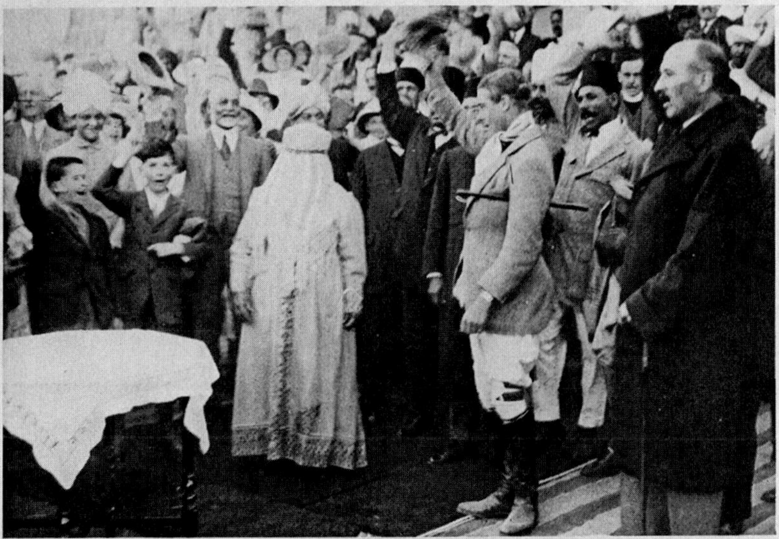

AT THE FINISH OF THE POLO TOURNAMENT, BHOPAL.

A GROUP TAKEN AT THE POLO GROUND, BHOPAL.

THE PRINCE WITH THE MAHARAJA PROCEEDING TO THE PALACE, GWALIOR.

ARRIVAL AT THE PALACE.

THE PROCESSION OF STATE ELEPHANTS, MEMBERS OF H.R.H'S SUITE DISMOUNTING AT THE PALACE, GWALIOR.

THE SON AND DAUGHTER OF THE MAHARAJA OF GWALIOR, NAMED AFTER KING GEORGE AND QUEEN MARY.

PRINCE GEORGE AND PRINCESS MARY OF 1ST GWALIOR INFANTRY MARCHING OUT OF THE PALACE.

PRINCE GEORGE AND PRINCESS MARY OF THE 1ST GWALIOR INFANTRY DRILLING WITH STALWART COMRADES OF THE REGIMENT.

PRINCE GEORGE AND PRINCESS MARY WITH TWO OFFICERS OF THE GWALIOR ARMY.

THE PRINCE BEING FITTED WITH A PAIR OF OVERSHOES AT FATEHPUR SIKRI.

PRESENTATIONS ON ARRIVAL AT DELHI.

UNVEILING OF KING EDWARD VII MEMORIAL, DELHI.

RULING PRINCES AT GARDEN PARTY, DELHI FORT.

L

DELHI. A PICTURESQUE GROUP AT THE GARDEN PARTY.

GARDEN PARTY AT THE FORT, DELHI.

AT THE INSPECTION OF THE 2ND BATT. SEAFORTH HIGHLANDERS, DELHI.

THE PRINCE CHATS TO WIVES AND FAMILIES OF THE N.C.O'S OF THE REGIMENT.

THE PRINCE IN THE UNIFORM OF THE 35/36 JACOBS HORSE, OF WHICH HE IS COLONEL-IN-CHIEF, DELHI.

THE MAHARAJA OF PATIALA.

A VETERAN SALUTES THE PRINCE, PATIALA.

PIG-STICKING, PATIALA.

ON ARRIVAL AT JAMMU—THE PRINCE AND MAHARAJA OF KASHMIR LEAVING THE STATION.

THE LAMA INSTRUMENTALISTS WHO PRODUCED WEIRD MUSIC, JAMMU.

PASSING THROUGH LINES OF SCHOOL-CHILDREN AT SERAI ALAMGIR.

IN THE KHYBER PASS.

A NATIVE OUTPOST ON THE FRONTIER OF AFGHANISTAN.

IN THE MALAKAND PASS. LEADING MEN OF THE SWAT TRIBE AT FORT CHAKDARA.

THE PRINCE MOUNTED ON 'VICTORY.'

THE PRINCE'S STAFF POLO TEAM IN INDIA.

A GURKHA SOLDIER'S FAMILY AWAIT THE ARRIVAL OF THE PRINCE.

OPENING THE MILITARY COLLEGE, DEHRA DUN.

TYPES OF GURKHA WOMEN WHO CAME TO GREET THE PRINCE AT DEHRA DUN.

THE UNVEILING OF THE BALUCH MEMORIAL AT KARACHI—THE PRINCE'S LAST CEREMONY BEFORE LEAVING INDIA.

THE ROYAL BARGE APPROACHING THE LANDING PLACE, COLOMBO.

ONE OF THE TRIUMPHAL ARCHES
ON THE ROUTE, COLOMBO.

GUESTS AT THE GARDEN PARTY,
KING'S PAVILION, KANDY.

KANDYAN NOTABLES BEING
PRESENTED TO THE PRINCE.

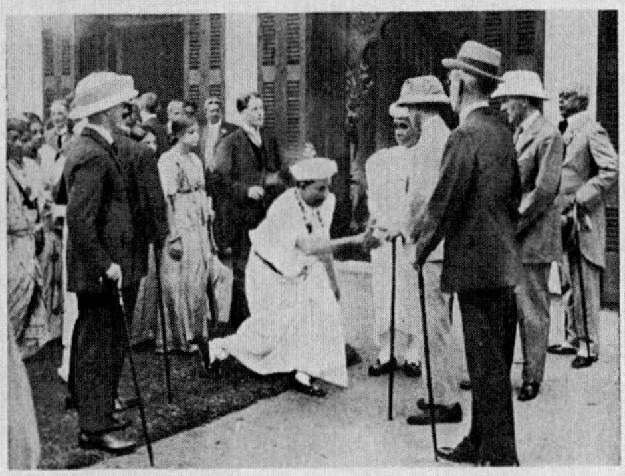

M

A DECORATED STREET AND TRIUMPHAL ARCH IN THE CHINESE QUARTER AT KUALA LUMPUR, FEDERATED MALAY STATES.

SCHOOL-CHILDREN ON THE ROUTE, KUALA LUMPUR.

PICTURESQUE CHILDREN IN THE STREETS OF KUALA LUMPUR.

A SECTION OF THE CHINESE COMMUNITY, KUALA LUMPUR, FEDERATED MALAY STATES

DYAK TRIBESMEN FROM BORNEO WELCOME THE PRINCE AT SINGAPORE.

DYAK WAR DANCES, SINGAPORE.

THE PRINCE UNVEILS THE STRAITS SETTLEMENTS WAR MEMORIAL, SINGAPORE.

DYAK WOMEN WHO CAME FROM BORNEO TO WELCOME THE PRINCE.

A DYAK WOMAN WITH THE SKULL OF A FALLEN ENEMY TRIBESMAN.

WILD MEN OF BORNEO AT SINGAPORE.

THE PRINCE CARRIED THROUGH THE STREETS IN A CHAIR BORNE BY CHINESE COOLIES, HONG-KONG.

SECTION OF A CHINESE PROCESSION, HONG-KONG.

THE PRINCE INSPECTS THE 102ND GRENADIERS, HONG-KONG.

JAPAN

NO Western Power ever received a foreign prince with greater enthusiasm than was shown by the Japanese people everywhere during this visit. The warmth of his welcome was almost overpowering. A nation that until only a little while before had looked upon cheering as an insult, and dead silence as the only proper way of saluting royalty, literally shouted itself hoarse. Peasants from the remote provinces, no less than the inhabitants of the cities, lifted their voices as readily and as lustily as the spectators in a London street. It might well be said that the Prince was carried across Japan on a torrent of cheers. Tiny children scarcely able to walk piped bravely with their elders ; old men to whom the present-day régime is still a little dazing, joined resolutely with the younger generation. It was rhythmic, well-disciplined cheering, punctuated with deep bows and the simultaneous waving of little British and Japanese flags. The tremendous social upheaval that has shaken Japan to its foundations was apparent in this nation-wide wave of feeling. Here was the voice of the East heard in no uncertain tones, giving vent in a Western way to its friendship and admiration for the nation's guest. The Prince is not likely to forget his progress from the quayside at Yokohama through four weeks of lavish hospitality to the final farewell scene at Kagoshima.

The journey from Yokohama to Tokio took him through

crowds that were practically continuous along a route 19 miles in length. His special train moved out of the harbour enclosure (where Japanese marines and soldiers formed a double guard of honour) into the massed population of the seaport, and the tumult of Yokohama merged imperceptibly with that of the industrial suburbs which link it with the capital. All the workers left the dockyards and factories to see him ; the trams stood still, and even the priests came from their temples to stand beside the railway with heads bent and eyes fixed reverently on the ground. The noise died away as the train entered Tokio central station, where the Prince Regent awaited his guest in solemn silence, standing aloof from a glittering assemblage of Imperial princes, officials of the household, cabinet ministers and all the high officers of the army and navy. Once clear of the station however, his Royal Highness was again overwhelmed by the cries of the people. From the broad square outside, which is the nucleus of the new European Tokio, to the modern Akasaka palace—a miniature Versailles—where he was lodged during his stay in the capital, he had a reception that could not be surpassed.

The first week was spent in the capital, and was devoted almost entirely to official functions, performed in accordance with the rigid etiquette of the Imperial Court. There were ceremonial calls on the Empress, and various members of the Imperial family; a series of state banquets, garden parties and receptions, and visits to public institutions. Whenever the Prince appeared in the streets he found them full of cheering people. The crowd seemed to spring up as if by magic, controlled by severe little policemen, always with its flags and its chorus of "Banzai," the Japanese form of "Hurrah." The morning after his arrival he drove through such a scene—smiles and shouts on all sides—to the University, where the students and the faculty were assembled in a pavilion in the grounds to see him presented with an address of welcome. After lunch, he was called to the balcony of Akasaka palace to hear 2,000 little boys and girls sing "God Save the King" in English, and to make them a little speech. On Good Friday he attended service at the Anglican church, and unveiled two tablets to the memory of former members of the British colony killed in the war. He saw the pick of the Japanese army at Yoyogi parade ground, in the suburbs of Tokio, where he reviewed a complete division of the Imperial Guard. On this occasion he wore the uniform of a Japanese general, and the Prince Regent and the members of the General Staff rode with him when he inspected the troops. He spent one morning at the Peace Exhibition, viewing the many industrial, commercial, and artistic exhibits collected from all parts of Japan, and the interesting contributions from foreign countries. Another public appearance was in Hibiya Park—the St. James's Park of Tokio—where 15,000 students greeted him with enthusiasm. On both occasions the Prince was profoundly impressed by the cordiality of his reception.

The entertainments given in his honour involved much labour and more expense. Two of the Prince's hosts thought nothing of building private theatres, solely for a single after-dinner performance. Count Uchida, the Foreign Minister, added a wing to the Foreign Office residence, which contained a large apartment of unpainted wood, decorated simply but very effectively in the Japanese style, with a low stage at one end. The Prince and his fellow guests were ushered into this beautiful room on the conclusion of dinner, and witnessed a performance by dancers from the Imperial Theatre, which was like a series of brilliant colour prints come to life in a garden filled with cherry-blossoms. The performers were artistes of the highest merit, and they were paid for two months solely to ensure their attendance on this occasion.

Baron Mitsui, one of the richest men in the world, put up a theatre in the courtyard of his Japanese mansion, which cost £30,000. It was built strictly according to the traditional design for the presentation of "No" plays, a form of dramatic art which was very popular with the nobles and feudal lords of old Japan. A kind of open pavilion of wood, approached by a covered gallery, constituted the stage ; a chorus sat on one side, and rendered appropriate music while the characters in historic costumes walked on and off with exaggerated gestures, and recited their parts in the affected voice demanded by the "No" drama.

The gala performance at the Imperial Opera House gave his Royal Highness an even more comprehensive view of the Japanese stage. So keen was the competition among the leading actors to appear on this occasion, that a programme lasting until after one o'clock in the morning was fully carried out, in order that as great a number of performers as possible might be included. The Opera House is built on European lines, and only the stage setting and arrangements for this performance were Japanese. The auditorium was an even more wonderful spectacle on this occasion than the stage. The Prince of Wales and the Prince Regent sat in arm chairs in the centre of the first row of the dress circle, with six Imperial Princesses in European costume on their right, and six Imperial Princes on their left. Around them were grouped the Ministers, high officers of state, and members of the Imperial Court. The theatre was filled to the last seat ; all the ladies were in evening dress, the men in uniforms covered with decorations; and such a scene had never before been witnessed even on gala nights. The appearance of the Imperial family almost *en masse* at a public theatrical performance was itself unprecedented. The plays presented covered various periods of the Japanese drama.

Two garden parties gave further opportunites for the Prince to meet the distinguished men of the Empire. The Imperial cherry blossom garden party, an annual festival of historic importance, was held in the park of Shinjoku palace. Unfortunately the cherry blossoms were not at their best, the season having begun earlier than usual, but the gardens looked very charming and the weather, fortunately, was fine. More than 9,000 guests were bidden to this gathering. The Empress—walking with the Prince, who was in the uniform of the Welsh Guards—led a little procession of Princesses and other members of the Imperial family, all in European dress, along the line of assembled guests, amid profound bows, and afterwards refreshments were served at open-air buffets. The afternoon had an unexpected and dramatic sequel. As the guests left the Palace grounds, they saw a heavy cloud of smoke enveloping the lower quarter of Tokio, and they came into an excited mob, surrounded by fire engines and fire "gods" held by Japanese, to find the Imperial Hotel in flames. Several members of the Prince's staff, and a number of officers of the *Renown* and the *Durban* were staying in the main building, and nearly all their belongings were lost. Only those guests fortunate enough to have had quarters in the annexe saved their luggage—thanks largely to the efforts of Marine orderlies from the *Renown*. The Minister of the Imperial Household went immediately to the scene and took charge of the homeless members of the Royal party; other accommodation was found for them, and the authorities showed the greatest solicitude in providing for their comfort. The Prince visited the scene of the fire next day.

The Marquis Inouye gave a garden party in the grounds of his delightful residence, at which many notable Japanese were present. Admiral Togo, the greatest hero in Japan, was the dominant figure, as he was at many other functions given in honour of the Prince. He always stood apart from the other guests, a silent, shy, little man in naval uniform, his eyes fixed meekly on the ground, and only looking up when someone was brought forward and presented. He smiled on one occasion when an English guest told him that in England he was called "the Nelson of Japan." Admiral Togo shook his head deprecatingly and continued to study the pattern of the lawn. The Marquis Inouye provided many diversions for his guests. He engaged famous artists and decorators of pottery to prepare souvenirs on the spot. They sat at little stands with piles of unbaked ware before them, ready to adorn a selected piece with a design in colours, after which it was put into a furnace and fired while the owner waited. A large temporary building was erected adjoining the wonderful rock garden solely for the service of refreshments, and twelve cooks were busy with an elaborate menu for afternoon tea. The family of the Marquis, in Japanese dress, received the Prince in the house.

The exhibition of netting wild duck in the Imperial preserve at Hama palace was one of the most unusual experiences of the Prince's stay in Tokio. After lunch in a little pavilion at the edge of a little lake, the Prince and the Prince Regent—both in tweeds—and the members of their suites, were conducted to the 700-year-old preserve. It is a lake carefully hidden from observation, and approached only by the keepers. From it radiate a series of miniature canals, each about 4 feet wide and 50 feet long, with the sides banked up to form a kind of low breastwork. At the end farthest from the lake is a bamboo screen pierced with narrow slits, through which observation can be kept. The duck are enticed from the lake into one of these smaller waterways by scattering a liberal supply of grain. The duck netters have previously been posted behind the screen, and they wait in silence until the keeper on watch gives the signal. When the waterway is full of eager duck, the netters creep forward swiftly, four along either breastwork, holding long poles to which are attached the nets. Simultaneously they reach over the breastwork; the startled duck rise, and the open nets are flung forward with a quick turn of the wrist in the effort to capture them. A falcon perched on the wrist of a keeper is ready to dart after any duck that flies inland, and bring it swiftly down. The Prince and the Regent entered into this sport with great zest, and went from one canal to another with varying success. Great skill is required to "flick" a fugitive duck into the net, and it is much harder than it seems to an onlooker.

The Prince's other engagements in Tokio included a dinner and a ball at the British Embassy; a state banquet at the Imperial palace, and his own dinner to the Prince Regent at the Akasaka palace at which other Princes and Princesses and many high officials were present.

One day was spent at Yokohama. His Royal Highness unveiled the Allied War Memorial in the General Cemetery, for which ceremony a guard was landed from the *Renown* by permission of the Japanese Government. This honour was deeply appreciated by the British community, for ordinarily no foreign troops are permitted to bear arms in Japanese territory. In the afternoon the Prince visited the Japanese fleet and went over the *Mutsu*. He dined in the flagship *Nagato*, and before going ashore to the ball given by the British community, saw a prodigal display of fireworks set off from the *Renown*. The final explosion seemed to envelop the entire ship in flame, and it was admittedly the finest effort of the kind ever witnessed by the admiring inhabitants of Yokohama.

When the Prince left Tokio for the interior, he found everywhere the same fervent enthusiasm. He travelled first to Nikko, celebrated for its beautiful temples, and the usual outpouring of villages marked the progress of his special train. Happy school children were collected in thousands at every wayside station; the mayor was there in a frock coat, supported by all the municipal officials, and flanked by rows upon rows of smiling women in their best kimonos; workers from the fields and prosperous factory owners at the head of their employees; Shinto priests; Buddhist priests; Christian missionaries leading the cheers of the mission schools; ex-soldiers, and prefectural authorities. This varied throng had few gaps, for even the labourers in the rice fields were gathered in groups beside the line. The Prince saw this stirring panorama in the sunshine of a perfect spring day, and at dusk he came into lantern-lit Nikko. One such journey in Japan was so like another, yet so different. The cheers and the flags and the mobilised townspeople arrayed so neatly beside the Royal train could be duplicated throughout the island wherever he went; yet each community made clear its individuality, and impressed upon the observer the distinctiveness of its welcome. Such receptions never grew monotonous.

At Nikko the Prince saw Toshu-gu, the mausoleum of Ieyasu, the first of the great Shoguns of the Tokugawa era. This the Japanese declare—not without truth—

SHOOTING THE RAPIDS (JAPAN)

to be the most perfect shrine in Japan. Although three centuries old, it is to-day intact and perfectly preserved. He spent one morning walking through the precincts of the other temples; he explored the quaint curio shops, and watched the flock of pilgrims toiling up the steep main street to the shrines beyond the Daiya river.

He made the difficult ascent to Lake Chuzenji and the famous Kegon waterfall, and on the way back bought a gnarled stick for Sir Harry Lauder. On the return journey to Tokio he motored from Nikko through the avenue of cryptomeria, celebrated throughout Japan, to Imaichi, finding the inevitable crowds on either hand. At Imaichi station, where he rejoined the Royal train, he was met by a delegation of high Shinto priests with kindly messages of farewell.

Four days were spent in the Hakone lake district, where the Prince had many varied views of the beautiful mountain Fuji-yama, a perfect cone which towers above the surrounding country and can be seen for many miles at sea. The journey to Hakone was made from Yokohama, after the conclusion of the Tokio visit. His Royal Highness lunched with the Prince Regent at the villa of Prince Kan-in, and drove up the narrow valley into the heart of the Hakone mountains—a favourite holiday resort for Europeans resident in Japan. Rain marred the excursions, and heavy banks of mist drifted over the mountains during the second day of his stay. He met the Prince Regent for the last time at a palace crowning the promontory overlooking Lake Hakone, where he said good-bye on April 24 before continuing his journey to Western Japan. Miyanoshita, one of the loveliest spots in Japan, was the Prince's headquarters for two days. He visited the Fujiya hotel, which at the time was full of tourists, and lunched with the other guests in the public room. The Fujiya hotel and the buildings in the vicinity rocked ominously in the earthquake of April 25, when considerable damage was done in Tokio. The Prince regretted that he did not experience the shock. He was motoring between Yumoto and Miyanoshita at the time, and knew nothing of it until afterward.

A week in and around Kyoto revealed the charm of old Japan. The Prince lived in the Omiya palace, one of the many Imperial buildings for which Kyoto is famous. His first act, on the day of his arrival, was to go to Momoyama, on the outskirts of the city, and lay a wreath on the tomb of the late Emperor Meiji, grandfather of the Prince Regent, under whom Japan emerged into the ranks of Western nations, and who is revered and worshipped by the entire nation.

Kyoto shows the effect of western civilisation less than other large cities of Japan. Its ancient monuments are carefully preserved, and the modern skyscraper type of office building which disfigures Tokio has not yet appeared. The Imperial palaces and the temples are Kyoto's chief glory. One can see to-day the actual apartments in the Nijo palace where the Shogun lived and held his court, and the Imperial palace, the residence of the Emperors of that day, who nominally ruled the country. The Prince went over both palaces, entering by the seldom-used Imperial gateway, and in that of the Emperor he saw the throne-room in which the coronation of the Prince Regent's father took place a few years ago. His Royal Highness also visited the Kinkakuji temple, or "golden pavilion," which is a monument of the Ashikaga period, and the wonderful Hongwan-ji temple, the fountain-head of Jodo Shinshu Buddhism. He went to the University and was entertained by the students in the Kamo gardens. The Governor of the province gave him a Japanese dinner. They sat together on cushions on the floor and ate strange dishes with chopsticks, and drank warm sake (rice wine) in the orthodox manner. The Prince was present at several other Japanese dinners in Kyoto and elsewhere. They were invariably accompanied by dances and songs, usually performed on a little stage. The room itself was of wood, with movable walls of glazed paper, and matting on the floor. The Mayor of Kyoto's dinner was served in European fashion in a building that was partly Japanese, partly European in design, and afterwards the Prince and the other guests were taken into the principal theatre of Kyoto, adjoining the dining hall, where the celebrated "Cherry Dance" was performed by pupils of the Geisha school.

The most interesting excursion from Kyoto was to Lake Biwa and thence to Gifu to see the cormorant fishing. The route lay through mountain roads lined with children as far as Otsu on the lake, where the Prince embarked in the *Midori Maru*, a little steamer which made her first trip in his honour. Lake Biwa is one of the "show" places of Japan; it is hemmed in by quaint little villages, with a background of snow-tipped mountains, and on this afternoon its placid surface was dotted with sail boats beflagged as though for a regatta, while on the shore were thousands of people waving a greeting to the Prince. Gifu, famous for its paper lanterns as well as its trained cormorants, sparkled with countless lights when his Royal Highness went out after sunset in a graceful low-roofed barge to watch the fishing on the Nagaragawa. It was a weird and wonderful sight. The cormorants fished as they have done at Gifu for the past 1,000 years. Ten long slender boats carried the fishermen and the birds. In the prow of each boat hung a basket of iron rods in which a fire of pinewood blazed fiercely. Near by stood the Master Fisher, in his skirt of rice straw and dark tunic, the dress in which his predecessors fished in the presence of the Emperor centuries before. In his left hand he held a dozen long cords which were tied to iron rings fastened low on the long necks of the cormorants. Each bird had its accustomed place at one side of the boat and would not fish willingly elsewhere. If changed to another position, it plainly showed its resentment. The cormorants dived repeatedly, amid the cries of the boatmen, and reappeared with fish in their beaks. The iron ring prevented their swallowing their prey which was deftly extracted by pressure on the throat.

On another day the Prince motored from Kyoto to Makeoka, and descended the Hozu rapids in a flat-bottomed barge. He sat in an arm chair, and the boatmen guided the boat dexterously among the rocks and around steep curves, as it plunged into a current like a millrace, and emerged into calm water, only to be seized a few minutes later by another rapid. It was an exciting and picturesque voyage lasting an hour and a quarter. The lower end of the narrow valley yielded the usual crowd of spectators perched on slippery rocks, and six deep along the wooded banks, increasing in numbers until the Prince's boat reached the landing place at Arashiyama. Here he was received by Count Otani, with whom he had tea in the grounds of the Count's country house.

From Kyoto the Prince went to Nara, the first permanent capital of Japan, which is remarkable to-day chiefly for its seven great Buddhist temples. At one of these, Horyu-ji, the oldest existing Buddhist temple in the Empire, he witnessed the "Miko," a sacred dance by young girls. At Todai-ji, the chief temple of the so-called Kegon sect, he was shown the gigantic image of Buddha, the "Nara-no-Daibutsu," 53½ feet high, which is the largest in the country, and near by the great bell, the deep, solemn notes of which are constantly resounding throughout the city. He fed the sacred deer which roam freely in a grove of tall cryptomerias at the Kasuga shrine, and spent some time in the Sho-shoin store-house, a museum 1,000 years old, which is filled with various articles connected with Buddhist worship: vestments, swords, books, manuscripts and children's playthings. A day and a half was all too short for an adequate view of the treasures of Nara.

Then came an abrupt transition from ancient to modern Japan. The Prince left Nara by tram, and an hour later entered Osaka, the bustling industrial centre which has been called the "Japanese Birmingham,"—a city of mills and factories overhung with smoke, altogether progressive, prosperous, and unlovely. The Royal visit lasted barely two hours, but the enthusiasm of Osaka's workpeople made it a memorable two hours. They surged around the Prince and ignored all efforts of the police to keep them at a distance; they followed him madly, shouting like an English football crowd, and both at the railway station and at the old Castle where he held a reception, they made it clear they were very glad to see him.

The voyage through the Inland Sea gave his Royal Highness a last look at rural Japan, and at places yet untouched by Western "progress." A new steamship, the *Keifuku Maru*, constructed for the mail service between Shimonoseki and Fusan (Korea), which had just left the builder's hands, was employed for this tour. It had been especially fitted and furnished for the Prince and his suite; the saloons were filled with masses of fresh flowers, curious dwarf trees, and singing birds in gilt cages, and servants of the Imperial Household replaced the ordinary staff of stewards. It was more like a luxurious private yacht than a passenger boat.

The voyage began at Kobe. The Prince arrived there from Osaka on the evening of Friday, May 5, and sailed early next morning. It was greatly regretted that he could spend only a few hours in Kobe, but the very full programme arranged for the last four days of his stay in Japan left no alternative. He went direct from the train, on arriving at Kobe, and held a brief reception at the Prefecture. There was just time to change for the Japanese dinner given in his honour by the Governor of Hiogo Prefecture. The Prince was received in a modern European mansion which had been taken for the occasion, and the Governor first entertained him with a curious marionette show, seen only in the Osaka district. Puppets dressed in the robes of ancient Japanese warriors, manipulated by men in black gowns and masks, danced and gesticulated in an amusingly life-like manner, on an improvised stage in the drawing-room. Women in Hokkaido costumes performed a slow, pleasing dance. Dinner was served in a Japanese pavilion adjoining the mansion. The Governor and his guests sat as usual on cushions, and the courses were arranged on low individual tables. A ball by the British community at the Oriental Hotel followed the dinner. The streets through which the Royal party drove were framed in red lanterns held by students as a barrier against the impetuous crowd. While the Prince danced, the people waited patiently along his route to the wharf, to give him a volley of farewell "Banzais" when he embarked at 1 a.m.

The Inland Sea yielded one surprise after another. Whenever the *Keifuku Maru* swung from mid-channel towards the shore, villagers could be seen massed compactly at the water's edge with flags and gestures of welcome. Flat-bottomed fishing boats ventured as near the steamer as possible, that their quaintly garbed crews might salute the Prince ; British and Japanese flags flew from their masts, and on every face was a smile. Sometimes a large schooner would put off with the entire population of a village on board, the school children packed tightly at the bows, the women amidships, and the men astern and clinging to the rigging. Peasants came from many miles inland to see the *Keifuku Maru* pass. They gave a demonstration that was little short of astounding when the Prince landed in the afternoon at Takamatsu, the principal port of the island of Shikoku. This landlocked harbour, surrounded by lofty hills, is dominated by the white walled castle of Tamamo-ju, built by the daiymo Ikoma, and now the seat of the Matsudaira family. The entire population of the island seemed to be concentrated in the streets of the town. Special trains followed each other into Takamatsu during the morning; some delegations had travelled all night, and each was complete with its school children, merchants, civic authorities, farmers, every person from the smallest boy to the oldest woman brandishing the British and Japanese colours as the Prince passed through their ranks. Such a welcome was usual in the towns near Tokio, but it was wholly unexpected in this remote locality.

While at Takamatsu, his Royal Highness was the guest of Count Matsudaira, whose ancestors were powerful Daiymos when the Shogunate was supreme, and who to-day is the overlord of Takamatsu. Count Matsudaira spent more than £10,000 in preparing for this half-day visit of the Prince, a fifth of which was devoted to building a special road to the top of the hill called Yashima, near the town. This is a place of great historical interest, the Taira clan having taken refuge here before the battle in which they were finally exterminated by Yoshitsune, the famous general of the Minamoto clan in 1185. A Buddhist temple on the summit contains many relics of the battle, and the priests were waiting to exhibit them to the Prince.

Count Matsudaira gave a portion of his estate, called

Ritsurin, as a public park for the people of Takamatsu, and here the Prince had tea and fished for carp in the little lake, while the crowd waited outside the gates. He planted a tree in commemoration of his visit, and saw many Japanese ex-soldiers. Then motoring to the foot of Yashima, he encountered another three mile strip of cheering humanity strung along the way. It overflowed into the green rice-fields and even reached the lower branches of roadside trees.

In the evening, Count Matsudaira gave a Japanese dinner in his mansion within the walls of the ancient castle. The province had been searched for the most beautiful and accomplished dancing girls to entertain the guests. More than three hundred servants were busy for a week preparing the dinner and the decorations. Famous actors performed a "No" play in which a demon disguised as a lovely woman tried to overpower the hero and his followers when they put to sea in a small boat. Twelve geishas, wearing silk kimonas especially woven for the occasion, in which Union Jacks and the Rising Sun were intermingled, gave a graceful dance peculiar to the province.

All this time the people of Takamatsu waited in the streets. When his Royal Highness left the castle precincts at 10 o'clock, he was ushered to his barge at the landing stage through a lane lit with coloured lanterns—each lantern held aloft by a sturdy member of the "Banzai" chorus, and he went back to the *Keifuku Maru* in the glare of harbour fireworks.

Next morning the steamer resumed her voyage through the populous Inland Sea, and in the afternoon anchored off the sacred island of Miyajima, one of the "three famous sights" of Japan. Its temples are visited annually by thousands of pilgrims. Dogs are not allowed

THE TORII IN THE INLAND SEA (JAPAN)

on the island ; births and deaths must not take place there, and according to an ancient custom, if a birth should occur unexpectedly, mother and child are sent to the mainland for 30 days. Sacred deer roam about and ask to be fed by visitors, and there is even a sacred horse that looks out longingly at the world. The chief temple of Itsuku-shima, which stands on a bluff above the village, is more than a thousand years old. The other buildings, including subsidiary shrines, oratories, and a treasure house are built partly on piles over the sea, and connected by open galleries. A magnificent Torii or arch, of massive wooden beams, stands in the sea as a kind of watergate ; it is a striking feature in a beautiful picture. Near the temples are quaint little shops which sell wooden toys of all kinds, and mementoes for pilgrims. After visiting the temples, the Prince spent some time buying souvenirs, unnoticed by the Japanese pilgrims who were haggling over the price of tin trumpets and wooden soldiers. The *Keifuku Maru* that night appeared to rest in a vast field covered with coloured flowers. Thousands of paper lanterns, each supported on a wooden base, were set afloat from the far shore and they drifted slowly across the windless bay until the placid surface was hidden under a mantle of glowing scarlet and green and orange. One could not have believed that such a beautiful effect could be secured with such simple, inexpensive materials.

After seeing Miyajima, the Prince spent a day with the Japanese Navy. He first travelled in the light cruiser *Kiso* from the anchorage of the *Keifuku Maru* at Miyajima, to the island of Etajima, to visit the Naval Academy—the Osborne of Japan. The cadets received him on the parade ground beside the jetty. They were sturdy, immobile youths with shaven heads and stern faces, and were clad in dark blue, tight-fitting uniforms. A quarter of an hour later they assembled in the body of the Great Hall, and when the Prince had come to the däis, the senior cadet stepped forward and made a brief speech of welcome in excellent English. The outstanding incident of the short visit was a curious competition on the exercise ground. Cadets, wearing thin white suits, assembled in two groups around two flagstaffs placed about one hundred feet apart. One portion of each contingent was banked solidly at the base of the staff, some of the cadets standing on the shoulders of the others, and the remainder constituted a kind of flying wedge which, at a signal from a bugle, dashed forward and tried to storm the opposite flagstaff. The opposing columns met midway with great force, and struggled on to the attack. The assaulting party sought to pull down the defenders by hammering them violently on the head, and then to remove the small flag which flew at the top of the staff. It was a hard, rough scrimmage in which shirts and trousers were torn to rags, and blood flowed freely. Three such assaults were delivered and then the battered cadets lined up again to cheer the Prince back to the *Kiso*.

From Etajima, the *Kiso* went to Kure, the great naval port and dockyard, an hour's journey through a torturous channel between the islands. The harbour was filled with saluting warships, including relics of the war with Russia and the latest type of cruisers. The majority of the inhabitants—and all the dockyard hands—were massed along the route to the Naval Commander-in-Chief's residence. After luncheon there, his Royal Highness went over the dockyard establishment. He saw object lessons in disarmament, inspired by the Washington Conference, which his hosts pointed out with mournful pride. Piles of new armour plate now useless, 16-inch guns fully mounted in their turrets, for the battleship *Kaga*, marked "scrap," and the hull of a battle cruiser which was being converted into an aeroplane carrier were displayed as evidences of Japan's good faith in adhering to the new programme for maintaining the world's peace. He was told that 40 per cent. of the dockyard personnel would have to be discharged because of this reduction in armaments.

The Prince re-embarked in the *Renown* in the afternoon, and sailed for Kagoshima, the last port of call in Japan. He landed there next morning, May 9. The visit to Kagoshima was of peculiar interest, for this seaport at the extreme tip of the island Empire played an important part in the upheaval which resulted in the final abandonment of Japan's anti-foreign policy in the middle of the last century. The powerful Satsuma Clan had resisted all efforts to throw open the country to foreign trade. An Englishman, named Richardson, was killed while trying to break through the train of the Daiymo Shimadzu Saburo, and to enforce the punishment of his murderers a British squadron bombarded Kagoshima in 1863. The family of Prince Shimadzu were the Prince of Wales' hosts at Kagoshima, and the descendants of the Satsuma clan prepared for him a reception that was second to none in warmth and enthusiasm.

For the last time he faced the deafening tumult of a Japanese crowd. Delegations from all parts of the Prefecture spent the day in Kagoshima town solely to welcome him ashore at 10 a.m., and see him sail again five hours later. His Royal Highness drove first to the ancestral shrine of the Shimadzu family, where boys in ancient costume, bearing short swords, sang a marching song, and men gave an exhibition of fencing. After lunch at Prince Shimadzu's villa, a company of archers in the traditional dress of Samurai, showed their skill in piercing small targets set against a distant bank. The Prince drove back to the harbour at 3 o'clock, and found it packed with people who had come to say good-bye. School children had the place of honour on the wharves. There must have been 8,000 of them waving flags and shouting as his Royal Highness stood beside his barge, surrounded by the representatives of the Imperial Court and the Government. Admiral Togo visited the *Renown* half an hour later, as did the members of the Prince's Japanese suite, to shake hands and receive his thanks for the nation's wonderful welcome.

When the *Renown* steamed out of the harbour, escorted by two light cruisers, small craft of all kinds surrounded her with volleys of "Banzais." Fishing boats overladen with excited spectators tried to join the procession seaward. From his saluting platform, the Prince watched a very inspiring scene as the crowded quays slowly melted in the mist, and the voice of Japan came fainter and fainter across the water. Two hours later he went back to his post above the bridge. The wind had risen, and rain drove in gusts against the *Renown* as she slipped between the widening arms of Kagoshima-wan bay. Her forward turrets and forecastle were hidden by bluejackets massed with their faces to starboard, as the cruisers ahead swung aside and turned back. On they came in the twilight, so close that their crews could be seen standing at attention. The *Renown's* band played "Auld Lang Syne," and from the passing ships came cheer after cheer, as caps were raised high in the air. Cheer answered cheer, and the Prince, bareheaded in the rain, waved his hand. The cruisers disappeared, steaming again towards Kagoshima, and the *Renown* made her course for the open sea.

HOMEWARD BOUND

THE homeward voyage was broken by seven calls. The Prince spent three pleasant days at Manila without any kind of formality. He was received on the morning of May 13, by General Leonard Wood, the Governor-General, and escorted to Malacanan Palace by American Cavalry. A dinner party and a dance were given in his honour; he played polo and thoroughly enjoyed himself.

On May 17, the *Renown* anchored in the landlocked harbour at Labuan, an island off the coast of Borneo, administered by the government of the Straits Settlements. The total white population is only 17, and the little town consists of a single main street of Chinese shops facing the harbour, and residential bungalows. Labuan was the headquarters for excursions up and down the coast, as the *Renown's* draught made it impossible for her to enter shallower harbours. The second day the Prince embarked in the escorting light cruiser *Cairo* and proceeded north to Jesselton, the capital of British North Borneo, where he spent an interesting three hours with wild tribesmen from the jungle. They had arranged an exhibition of "scurry" racing, in which the competitors are mounted on ponies, and the best man wins any way he can. The Dyaks showed him their expertness with their blowpipes. Their propensity for using poisoned arrows in settling feuds is so notorious that before being admitted to the enclosure where the Prince witnessed their feats of marksmanship, each man had to submit to having his arm scratched by one of his own darts to prove they were harmless. The blowpipes were of varying lengths up to six feet, of hard wood lined with tightly packed cotton wool. The Dyaks were able to hit a bulls-eye up to thirty yards with unfailing accuracy. They were very shy and suspicious. When the winner of the "scurry" race was brought up to be photographed he resisted fiercely, shouting, "Am I a woman that I should be mocked ? "

The Prince went next day from Labuan to Brunei, a native state on the coast of Borneo, south of Labuan, again travelling in the *Cairo* as far as the mouth of the river, and completing the journey to the capital—some 20 miles up stream—in a launch. The native houses are clustered on piles over the water, and some travellers call Brunei "the Venice of the East." The Prince was met at the landing stage by the Sultan and his suite, with an enormous palanquin, which was like a miniature bungalow slung on poles. Two chairs were placed under the canopy for the Prince and the Sultan, and thus enthroned they were borne in state by thirty panting warriors to the modest little Durbar Hall.

Penang was visited on May 23rd. The Prince made the journey in a tug from the *Renown's* anchorage 18 miles below the harbour, and he was received on landing by the entire population. The usual holiday had been proclaimed, and the crowd—Chinese and Malays, as well as the planters and officials from "up country" with their wives and families—spent most of the afternoon hurrying from one part of the town to another, in order to follow his Royal Highness on his rounds. He lunched at the Penang Club, and motored in and around Penang until it was time to re-embark in the tug at 7 o'clock.

The next port of call was Trincomalee, on May 27. The *Renown* was to have put in at Colombo for four days, but the monsoon had broken, and the harbour authorities would not advise bringing in a ship of her size, so she was deflected to the former naval station, on the north-east coast. The change was not unwelcome. Trincomalee, is remote from the busy world—the nearest railway station is 60 miles away, and the only mail of the day comes over the hills by omnibus—but this little town is very picturesque and restful, and the ships' company had plenty of opportunity for sport. The Prince went to Colombo by car and special train and spent two days there, returning on the morning of sailing, May 30.

The most desolate place visited during the entire tour was Great Hanish, an arid uninhabited rock in the Red Sea, where the *Renown* stopped June 5-6, to replenish her oil tanks. The Prince went ashore at daybreak and shot an antelope.

The visit to Cairo was devoid of ceremonial. His Royal Highness travelled by special train from Suez on the afternoon of June 9, and at every station in the desert between Suez and Ismailia, the natives were assembled to see him ; the British garrison at Ismailia was represented along the line, and aeroplanes flew over his saloon until nightfall. Zagazig, the largest town on the route, mustered hundreds of curious spectators in the streets adjoining the railway station, and his Royal Highness' reception was in every sense a friendly one. While in Cairo he stayed with Lord Allenby at the Residency. He lunched with the King of Egypt, made various excursions in and around the city, and left for Port Said late on the evening of the 11th.

Gibraltar was the last port of call. The Prince spent June 17 ashore, and went about the "Rock" without any ceremony. The *Renown* sailed that evening. She came up the coast of Spain and across the Bay in good weather, saluted by innumerable craft, and bombarded by hundreds of wireless greetings; and at 3 o'clock on the afternoon of June 20, 1922, the Eddystone rose out of a placid sea and showed her the way to Plymouth Sound.

THE PRINCE WITH PRINCE HIGASHI-FUSHIMI LANDING IN JAPAN.

LANDING IN JAPAN. MEMBERS OF THE BRITISH EMBASSY AND CONSULAR STAFFS PRESENTED TO THE PRINCE AT YOKOHAMA.

JAPANESE SCHOOL-CHILDREN WHO CHEERED THE PRINCE ON THE QUAY, YOKOHAMA.

THE PRINCE MET BY THE PRINCE REGENT OF JAPAN ON ARRIVAL AT TOKYO.

JAPANESE CHILDREN AT TOKYO WEARING BADGES COMPOSED OF THE BRITISH AND JAPANESE FLAGS.

A SECTION OF THE CROWD AWAITING ARRIVAL OF THE PRINCE, TOKYO.

THE PRINCE IN THE UNIFORM OF A JAPANESE GENERAL, TOKYO.

AT THE REVIEW, THE PRINCE AND THE PRINCE REGENT OF JAPAN PASSING DOWN THE LINE, TOKYO.

AT THE REVIEW TOKYO. RIGHT TO LEFT, H.R.H. THE PRINCE OF WALES, PRINCE KANIN, PRINCE REGENT OF JAPAN, COUNT CHINA.

AT THE IMPERIAL UNIVERSITY, TOKYO.

IN THE GROUNDS OF THE IMPERIAL UNIVERSITY, TOKYO.

AT THE IMPERIAL CHERRY GARDEN PARTY, TOKYO. H.R.H. WITH H.M. THE EMPRESS OF JAPAN, PRINCE REGENT ON LEFT AND PRINCE HIGASHI FUSHIMI ON RIGHT.

THE DEEP BOW OF SALUTATION—THE JAPANESE WAY OF MEETING

DUCK NETTING AT HAMA PALACE, TOKYO. THE PRINCE TESTS HIS SKILL.

DUCK NETTING. H.R.H. INTERESTED IN THE FALCON WHICH RETRIEVES ANY DUCK ESCAPING THE NETS.

THE PRINCE ON THE LAKE AT HAMA PALACE, TOKYO.

SELECTING A NET.

THE PRINCE OF WALES AND THE PRINCE REGENT OF JAPAN TAKE PART IN A FOURSOME OF GOLF AT TOKYO.

THE PRINCE OF WALES WATCHING THE PRINCE REGENT PUTTING.

H.R.H. PUTTING. THE PRINCE REGENT IS ON THE LEFT OF THE PICTURE.

THE PRINCE AND THE PRINCE REGENT OF JAPAN AFTER A ROUND OF GOLF.

THE PRINCE PURCHASES A WALKING STICK, LAKE CHUZENJI, NEAR NIKKO.

SHINTO PRIESTS IN THEIR PICTURESQUE ROBES, NIKKO.

THE PRINCE AT THE UNVEILING OF THE ALLIED FORCES WAR MEMORIAL, YOKOHAMA.

MOUNT FUJIYAMA FROM THE TOP OF LONG TRAIL PASS.

A GLIMPSE OF THE SNOW-CAPPED MOUNT FUJIYAMA.

DURING THE CRUISE ON LAKE BIWA THE PRINCE INSPECTS A LAKE-FISHING NET.

A VIEW OF LAKE BIWA FROM THE RAMPARTS OF HIKONE CASTLE.

AT A RUGBY FOOTBALL MATCH BETWEEN BRITISH AND JAPANESE TEAMS, KYOTO.

PLAYERS OF AN OLD TIME FOOTBALL GAME KNOWN AS 'KEMARI' AT KYOTO.

JAPANESE SCHOOLGIRLS PROUDLY DISPLAYED A UNION JACK DURING THE PRINCE'S VISIT AT KYOTO.

'SHOOTING THE RAPIDS' IN THE HOZUGAWA RIVER. H.R.H. IS SEEN WAVING A JAPANESE FLAG.

WHILST ON A SHOPPING EXPEDITION IN KYOTO THE PRINCE DISMISSES HIS MOTOR CAR AND HAILS A RICKSHAW.

THE PRINCE ON THE OBSERVATION PLATFORM OF THE ROYAL TRAIN, KYOTO—NARA.

FEEDING THE SACRED DEER IN NARA PARK.

A SACRED DANCE PERFORMED BY MIKO DANCERS.

THE GIANT BELL OF NARA, CAST IN THE YEAR 732 AND WEIGHS NEARLY 50 TON.

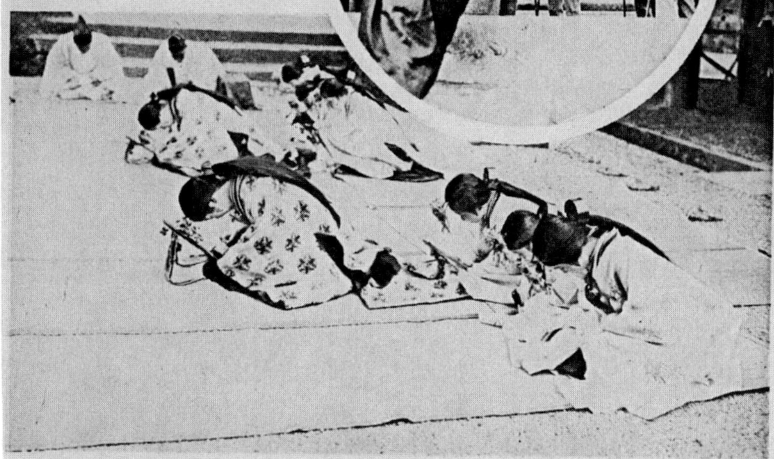

MIKO DANCERS AT THE KASUGA SHRINE, NARA.

FISHING IN THE LAKE OF RITSURIN PARK.

THE PRINCE FEEDING CARP IN RITSURIN PARK, TAKAMATSU.

THE PRINCE EXPERIENCES A RIDE IN A KAGO—AN ANCIENT FORM OF CONVEYANCE, TAKAMATSU.

AFTER PLANTING A TREE IN RITSURIN PARK, TAKAMATSU, THE THOUGHTFUL JAPANESE PROVIDE THE PRINCE WITH FACILITIES FOR WASHING.

THE PRINCE WALKING INTO THE VILLAGE OF JASHIMA.

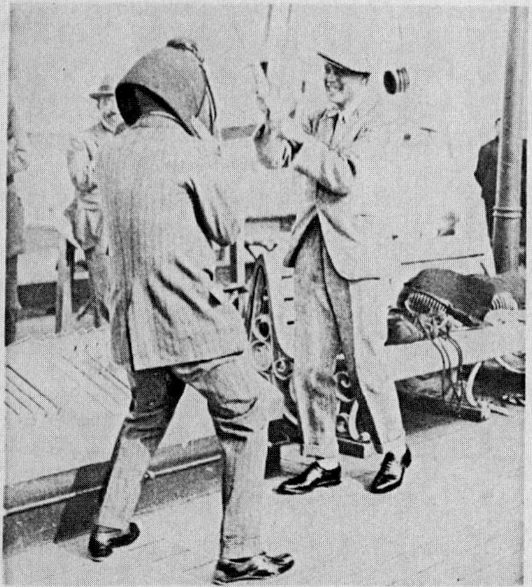

THE PRINCE TRIES THE EFFECT OF A BLOW WITH A FENCING STICK ON THE HEAD OF ONE OF HIS JAPANESE STAFF.

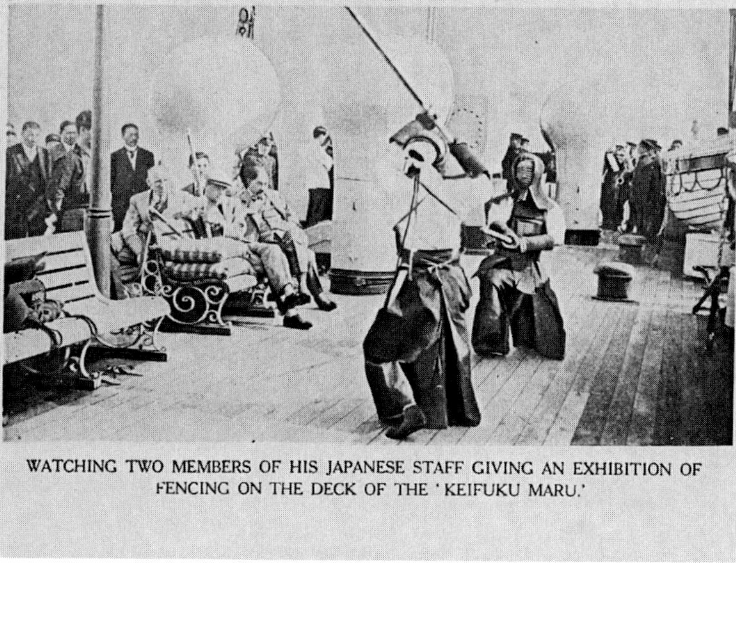

WATCHING TWO MEMBERS OF HIS JAPANESE STAFF GIVING AN EXHIBITION OF FENCING ON THE DECK OF THE 'KEIFUKU MARU.'

PLANTING A TREE IN THE TEMPLE AT MIYAJIMA (INLAND SEA).

THE GREAT TORII OF MIYAJIMA.

AT THE ROYAL NAVAL CADET SCHOOL, ETAJIMA, JAPANESE CADETS PLAYING THE GAME OF 'BOTAOSHI.'

THE PRINCE IN A GROUP AT THE NAVAL CADET SCHOOL.

A PARADE OF JAPANESE BOYS WHO GAVE A MARCHING DISPLAY ACCOMPANIED BY SONGS AT KAGOSHIMA.

ARCHERS AT PRINCE SHIMADZU'S VILLA, KAGOSHIMA.

THE PRINCE'S ARRIVAL AT PENANG.

THE PRINCE AND KING FUAD OF EGYPT IN THE GROUNDS OF ABDINE PALACE, CAIRO.

ON THE WAY HOME. H.R.H. WITH THE OFFICERS AND SHIP'S COMPANY OF H.M.S. 'RENOWN'

THE PRINCE MET BY THE DUKE OF YORK ON ARRIVAL AT PLYMOUTH.

PRINCE CHARLES OF BELGIUM AND COMMANDER DRUMMOND OF THE 'RENOWN.'

THE PRINCE AND THE DUKE OF YORK ON THE QUARTERDECK OF THE 'RENOWN.

LEAVING PADDINGTON STATION AFTER HIS RETURN FROM HIS INDIAN AND EASTERN TOUR